FIBONACCI TRADING

How to Master the Time and Price Advantage

CAROLYN BORODEN

New York   Chicago   San Francisco   Lisbon
London   Madrid   Mexico City   Milan   New Delhi
San Juan   Seoul   Singapore   Sydney   Toronto

8 9 0   QFR/QFR   1 5 4 3

ISBN: 978-0-07-149815-9
MHID: 0-07-149815-X

This publication is designed to provide accurate and authoritative information in regard to the subject matter covered. It is sold with the understanding that the publisher is not engaged in rendering legal, accounting, or other professional service. If legal advice or other expert assistance is required, the services of a competent professional person should be sought.

—*From a declaration of principles jointly adopted by a committee of the American Bar Association and a committee of publishers.*

McGraw-Hill Education books are available at special quantity discounts to use as premiums and sales promotions, or for use in corporate training programs. To contact a representative, please visit the Contact Us pages at www.mhprofessional.com.

This book is dedicated to my soldier
Lt. Col. Steven M. King who
was deployed to Afghanistan
while I wrote this book.

Thankfully, he is now home safe and retired from the US military!

CONTENTS

FOREWORD

Most traders have been exposed to some aspect of what we call Fibonacci trading, mostly in reference to Fibonacci price retracements. Traders have been using these retracements for years to help identify them price support and resistance. But Fibonacci retracements are just a beginner's application of these important ratios for trading. It is how you use them in different trading situations that is important. In addition, there are other geometric and harmonic ratios that are equally important that you will learn about in this book.

What most traders have never been taught is how to use these ratios for support and resistance time targets in the same manner as they are used for price targets. When you combine Fibonacci time and price projections as part of a trading plan, you should have a powerful approach to identifying trade opportunities. I don't think there is anyone who is more qualified to teach you about Fibonacci time and price trading strategies than the FibQueen herself (aka Carolyn Boroden).

I first met Carolyn in 1989 at the first *Gann-Elliott Magazine* (since evolved into *Traders World* magazine) conference in Chicago. She was one of the first people to study my Gann Home Study Trading Course, which was first released at that conference. But she wasn't new to the financial markets and trading in 1989. Unlike most trading educators, Carolyn has spent her entire adult life working with the financial markets, from floor runner as a teenager to fund advisor to day-trading mentor. While she has been a relentless student of the markets, she has also had years of practical experience in almost every phase of the trading business.

We kept in contact for several years after 1989, faxing charts, analysis, and trade strategies back and forth between Tucson and Chicago. In 1993, I convinced her to move to Tucson to work with me. She was soon wooed away by an offer to provide analysis and trade strategies for a fund for a whole lot more money than I was paying her, but we have remained friends and associates ever since.

She has been a student of my Dynamic Trading methods for almost 20 years and has used my Dynamic Trading software, which you will see in this book, since Version 1 was released in 1997. There is no better example of a relationship in which the "student becomes the teacher" than that of Carolyn and me. In recent years, I've learned as much from her as she did from me in the early years, especially about her symmetry setups and trade strategies, which you will learn in this book.

I'm very proud to have been her mentor in the early years and her friend forever, and I know that her book, which you hold in your hands, will be one of your most valuable reference books for your business of trading.

ROBERT MINER
Dynamic Traders Group, Inc.
Steamboat Springs, CO

ACKNOWLEDGMENTS

I would like to thank my many teachers over the years. First my mentor, Robert Miner, whom I met at a conference at the Midland Hotel in Chicago just after the market crash of 1987. Others who have contributed to my education over the years include Robert Krausz (who talked me into going to the conference where I met my mentor), Larry Pesavento, Bryce Gilmore, David Patterson, Mark Douglas, and Woodie of woodiescciclub.com.

Thank you to my new business associates John Carter and Hubert Senters and the Tradethemarkets.com group for their help and support in marketing and growing my business.

I would like to thank Richard Karst, aka RMK, for backing me up in my chat room so that I could sometimes have a life! Thank you, John Haytol, for the computer advice and vision of a virtual chat room with live charts. I would also like to thank Todd Phillips for helping me implement this vision with computer screen-sharing technologies that have forever changed my chat room. Thanks to Richard Lowrance for believing in me and supporting my work. Thanks to my friend Joe Nicholas of Hedge Fund Research, who must have thought I had "something going on" since he kept a business file on me! Thank you, William M. Kidder, aka "Uncle Bill," for giving me a chance to prove myself at DLJ when I was 18 at my first job on Wall Street!

I would also like to acknowledge my friend and client, Dr. Firouz Amirparviz, who left us in December 2004. I want to thank him and his family for treating me as if I was part of their family or, as he called it, for "adapting" me.

Last but not least, I would like to thank the entire King family for their love and support, especially during the task of writing this book. After all, a Queen needs her Kings! This family truly helped me keep my sanity when I overworked myself almost to the brink of a nervous breakdown. Love you all!

CB
aka Fibonacci Queen

INTRODUCTION

My purpose in writing this book is to give you an introduction to the fascinating world of Fibonacci. It is also to provide you with a very specific trading methodology that can be added to your current list of strategies. For me, this method has continued to identify key trading opportunities in the markets since 1989, and it has never failed me.

Chapter 1 will introduce you to the Fibonacci numbers and the Golden Ratio—the backbone of this methodology. Chapters 2 through 9 will take you through the steps of using Fibonacci on the price axis of the market, including the trade setups that are created with this work. (These are the trade setups that I provide for my clients every day in my live chat room.)

Chapters 10 to 13 explain how to apply Fibonacci to the time axis of the market and then combine this with the price work to find the highest-probability trade setups. Chapters 14 to 16 will help you fine-tune your market entries, ending with an example of a trade setup from analysis to entry. Last but not least, Chapter 17 focuses on trading psychology, discipline, money management, and the importance of having a written trading plan. (The proper psychology will allow you to implement your trading plan, with the discipline to follow the plan along with proper money management techniques.)

Like having a good starting hand in a game of Texas Hold 'Em, this book will teach you how to stack the market odds in your favor.

FIBONACCI TRADING

1 CHAPTER

FIBONACCI NUMBERS AND THE GOLDEN RATIO

For those who are not already familiar with the name Fibonacci, you may remember hearing something about it in 2006, when the movie *The DaVinci Code* appeared in theaters. When Jacques Saunière was found murdered at the Louvre Museum in Paris, the strange position that this deceased character was placed in mimicked the famous painting of the *Vitruvian Man* by Leonardo da Vinci. This painting has been known to illustrate how Fibonacci ratios appear in the human form. The film also piqued the curiosity of some people when the characters in the film started talking about Fibonacci numbers as part of a clue or code of some sort. For myself, I only chuckled and thought, "It's about time someone is taking Fibonacci seriously."

The Fibonacci number series and the properties of this series were made famous by the Italian mathematician Leonardo de Pisa. The Fibonacci number series starts with 0 and 1 and goes out to infinity, with the next number in the series being derived by adding the prior two. For example, 55 + 89 = 144, 89 + 144 = 233, 144 + 233 = 377, and so on (see the following number series):

0, 1, 1, 2, 3, 5, 8, 13, 21, 34, 55, 89, 144, 233, 377, 610, 987 . . . out to infinity

What is most fascinating about this number series is that there is a constant found within the series as it progresses toward infinity. In the relationship between the numbers in the series, you will find that the ratio is 1.618, or what is called the Golden Ratio, Golden Mean, or Golden or

Divine Proportion. (For example, 55 x 1.618 = 89, and 144 is 1.618 times 89.) Take any two consecutive numbers in the series after you get beyond the first few and you will find the Golden Ratio. Also note that the inverse or reciprocal of 1.618 is 0.618.

There are quite a few Web sites that are devoted to this number series and its properties. Just type the word *Fibonacci* into your favorite search engine and you'll be amazed at the wealth of information that exists on this subject.

The Golden Ratio can be found in many different places. The 1.618 ratio is used in architecture in what is called the "golden rectangle," as it is known to be pleasing to the eye. There are actually plastic surgeons who use these ratios to help them sculpt faces of "perfect proportion." You can also find the ratio in nature. It can be seen in flowers, the nautilus shell, ammonite fossils, and many other places. What I find to be most fascinating is that this ratio shows up in the pentagram (see Figure 1-1), which is known as a symbol for hidden occult knowledge. It occurred to me that maybe the ratio within the pentagram held a hidden secret to the market!

At one point in my education, I actually studied Jewish mysticism. One of my teachers from a Golden Dawn temple in California handed me a copy of a Disney cartoon called "Donald in Mathmagic Land," saying that I might enjoy it. Another student had brought it to his attention, as Donald Duck had a pentagram inscribed on his hand in this Disney cartoon. In this cartoon, which was produced to teach children about math, Donald Duck was on an adventure in Mathmagic land, where

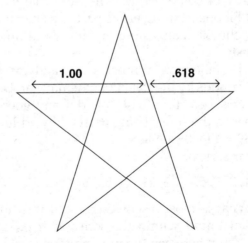

1.00   .618

F I G U R E   1 - 1

he visited with Plato and Pythagoras, talked about "secret mathematical societies," and learned about the Golden Section. The cartoon illustrated where the ratios of 0.618 and 1.618 exist in nature and architecture. This cartoon, which Disney released in 1959, is still available via the Internet, and it is well worth watching. The quote at the end of the cartoon was from Galileo, "Mathematics is the alphabet in which God has written the universe." I believe this to be true. If you study the "code" of the Fibonacci numbers and the ratios derived from this number series long enough, I think you will begin to agree with, or at least understand, that statement. This is *not* something that should just be blindly accepted because I have found it to be true. It is something that you must discover and then prove to yourself on your own journey!

What is important to *most* traders is that applying these ratios can help identify key support and resistance zones in the market, and therefore determine key trading opportunities or setups. I will show you how to apply these ratios in any market with adequate data. Thus, the application can give you a huge *edge* as a trader, if you use the techniques properly.

2 CHAPTER

APPLYING FIBONACCI RATIOS TO THE PRICE AXIS OF THE MARKET

We will not use the Fibonacci number series to analyze the markets. Instead, we will use the ratios derived from this number series. We've already discussed 1.618 and 0.618 or the Golden Ratio and its inverse. The main ratios I use in my everyday analysis are 0.382, 0.50, 0.618, 0.786, 1.00, 1.272, and 1.618.

I will sometimes also include 0.236, 2.618, and 4.236.

In Chapter 1, you saw how we found the 0.618 and 1.618 ratios within the Fibonacci number series, but what about the rest of these ratios? Well, actually, they are all related mathematically.

For example:

$$1.0 - 0.618 = 0.382$$
$$0.618 \times 0.618 = 0.382$$
$$1.0 \div 2 = 0.50$$
$$\text{Square root of } 0.618 = 0.786$$
$$0.618 \text{ is the reciprocal of } 1.618$$
$$\text{Square root of } 1.618 = 1.272$$
$$0.618 - 0.382 = 0.236$$
$$0.382 \times 0.618 = 0.236$$
$$1.618 \times 1.618 = 2.618$$
$$2.618 \times 1.618 = 4.236$$

Now what do we do with these ratios and how do they help us trade?

We will find our trade setups or trading opportunities by applying the main Fibonacci ratios on the price axis of the market. There are three basic trade setups that I use in my chat room every day: (1) price cluster setups, (2) symmetry setups, and (3) two-step pattern setups.

Author Tip This type of Fibonacci price analysis can work well in any market and pretty much on any time frame, as long as there is adequate data and you can identify key swing highs and lows on the chart. Do not attempt to use this type of analysis on something like a penny stock, where you can't identify any meaningful swings, or in a market with minimal data available. In such cases, this technique will have no value.

TOOLS OF THE TRADE

Since you are looking into this type of technical analysis, I am assuming that you have a computer; a market data source such as e-signal, quote.com, or Genesis Financial data; and a technical analysis program to manipulate the data. You *can* do some of this work by hand with paper charts and a calculator or a proportional divider, although it is tedious and not practical. (While I started the technical analysis phase of my career using those old-fashioned tools, I do *not* recommend that to anyone, given all the wonderful technology that is available today.)

The technical analysis program that I primarily use to run my time and price work is Dynamic Trader, with an e-signal feed as my data source. There are other programs that will run at least the price analysis work, though there are only a few that have both the proper price and time tools you will need if you choose to analyze both dimensions of the market.

Unless otherwise specified, most of the chart examples in this book are produced with the Dynamic Trader software. Also note that some of the charts may appear "fuzzy," or you may feel that you can't read the prices very clearly. Don't worry; I did not use a bad graphics program to capture these chart illustrations. This happens because the price relationships are clustering and essentially overlapping one another, making the chart levels difficult to read. This is something that we actually *want* to see happen. This will all make sense to you by the time you get through the first half of this book.

FIBONACCI PRICE RELATIONSHIPS

We start by running three different types of Fibonacci price relationships to find our trade setups. These are *retracements, extensions,* and *price projections* (sometimes called *price objectives*). First we will look at each of these types of price relationship individually. Later, we will be putting them together while we look for our trade setups. Each of these price relationships will be setting up potential *support* or potential *resistance* in the chart you are analyzing.

The definition of *support* is a price area below the current market where you will look for the possible termination of a decline and where you would consider being a buyer of whatever market you are analyzing. You might be looking to buy at or around support either to initiate a new trade on the long side *or* to exit a short position if you think the support may hold and the market won't decline any further.

The definition of *resistance* is a price area above the current market where you would look for the possible termination of a rally and consider being a seller. You might be looking to sell at or around resistance to initiate a new trade on the short side *or* to exit a long position if you think the resistance may hold and the market won't go any higher.

In the next three chapters, you will discover the types of price relationships that are necessary for running your analysis. Please do not get overwhelmed with the information I am presenting throughout this book. Be patient with yourself. If you start by applying one concept at a time, you will be well rewarded for your perseverance.

3 CHAPTER

FIBONACCI PRICE RETRACEMENTS

Fibonacci price retracements are run from a prior low-to-high swing using the ratios 0.382, 0.50, 0.618, and 0.786 (0.236 is also used in some cases if the swing is relatively long) to identify possible support levels as the market pulls back from a high. Retracements are also run from a prior high-to-low swing using these same ratios, looking for possible resistance as the market bounces from a low.

Most basic technical analysis packages will run the retracement levels for you when you choose the swing you want to run them from and select the proper Fibonacci price tool within the program you are using. If you want to understand the math, however, multiply the length of the swing (from low to high or from high to low) by the retracement ratios and then subtract the results from the high if you are running low-to-high swings, or add the results to the low when you are running high-to-low swings.

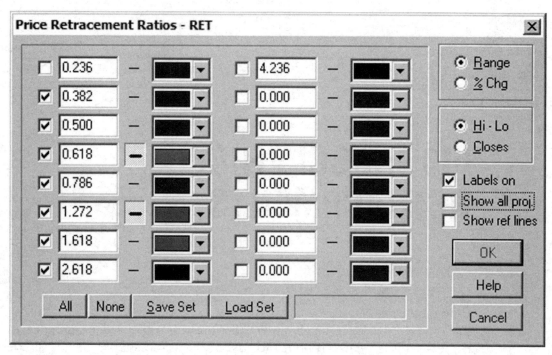

FIGURE 3-1

Figure 3-1 shows you the Price Retracement/Extension tool setup on Dynamic Trader that I have used to run the following price retracement examples. Note that I have selected in the setup box the ratios that I will be using to run both price retracements and price extensions (which will be illustrated in the next chapter). The same tool is used because both retracements and extensions are run from two points on a chart—either a high to a low or a low to a high. Since the mathematics of the program uses only these two points, we can use the same tool to run the price extensions of prior swings.

Note: All price retracements on the Dynamic Trader chart examples will be labeled as RET for retracements by the program.

Now that you have an idea of the type of Fibonacci tool you might use for your work, let's go through some retracement examples to help you understand what you might look for on a chart. Figure 3-2 is an example of the daily gold futures February 2007 contract. We ran the Fibonacci retracements from the 10/4/06 low to the 12/1/06 high, which was an 86.90-point swing, looking for potential support. Notice that this contract found support only around the 0.618 retracement of this prior swing. None of the other ratios provided any meaningful support.

FIGURE 3-2

This next retracement example is on a FOREX chart. My experience in this business has mostly been in the futures industry, including commodities, with a focus on the financial futures markets. I have also found this type of analysis valid for cash indexes, individual stocks, and the FOREX markets. On the daily euro chart (see Figure 3-3), we ran the retracement of the 12/4/06 high to the 12/18/06 low, looking for possible resistance levels. In this case, the euro found resistance first at the 0.618 retracement and then at the 0.786 retracement of that same swing.

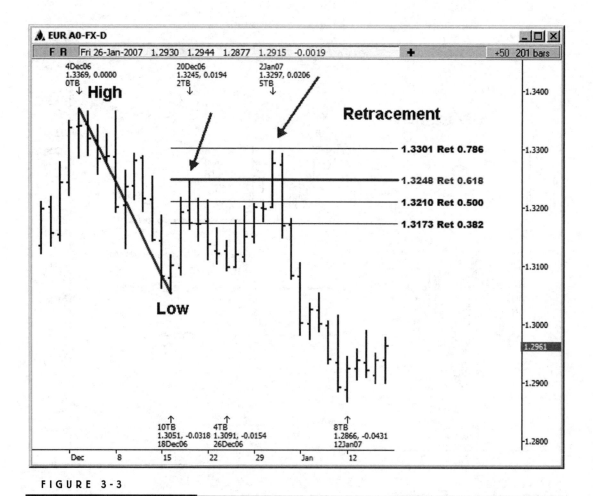

FIGURE 3-3

Our next retracement example is on a 15-minute mini-sized Dow chart (see Figure 3-4). Here the retracement was run from the high made on 1/17/2007 at 1:15 p.m. central time to the low made on 1/19/2007 at 8:45 a.m. central time. Here we were looking for possible resistance on the way back up from the 1/19 low. Notice that there are multiple swings within the larger swing that we measured for these price relationships. In later examples, we will run multiple retracements from these multiple swings. In this example, there was a minor move off the 0.382 retracement on the way up, but a much more important reversal against the 0.618 retracement level.

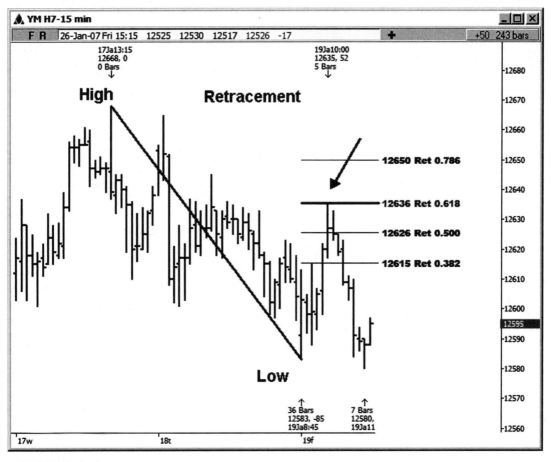

FIGURE 3-4

Figure 3-5 is another retracement example in the mini-sized Dow contract on a 45-minute chart. This is an example of a swing that is long enough (243 points) to include 0.236 in the retracement levels projected. Here we were looking for potential support. In this case, we saw a minor bounce off the 0.236 retracement, then a more healthy move off the 0.382 retracement. This example also illustrates that we will not always see perfect hits of Fibonacci levels. As long as they are relatively close, however, they are still considered valid.

Relatively close is generally 3 to 4 ticks in price above or below the actual projection level. For example, in this case, the low of 12482 made near the 0.382 retracement was 4 ticks below the actual retracement level of 12486. In some other markets, such as FOREX, I might allow a little

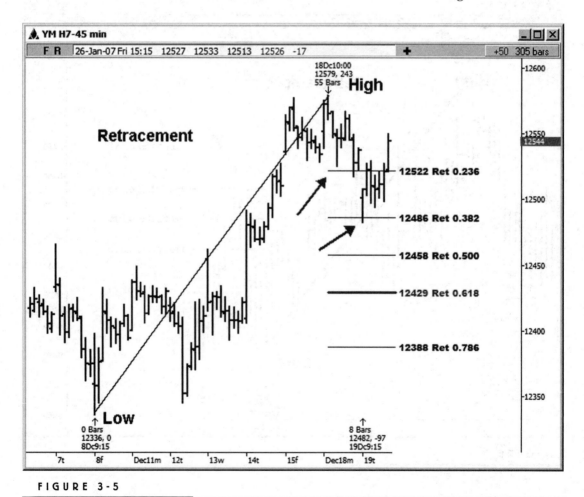

FIGURE 3-5

bit more leeway, especially if you are running the retracements from a rather large swing.

> **Author Tip** As a rule of thumb, a good way to judge whether or not a level should still be considered valid is to just look at the chart you are analyzing. If you don't see a glaring violation or shortfall of the level, I would still consider it valuable and leave it on the chart.

This next retracement example is on a daily chart of Microsoft (see Figure 3-6). Here we retraced the move from the 11/15/04 high at 27.50 to the 3/29/05 low at 23.82 looking for possible resistance on the way back up. Note that the 0.618 retracement was the only one that produced

FIGURE 3-6

a change in trend on this chart. The high was made exactly at the retracement at 26.09. You can't always expect perfect hits using these price relationships. However, don't be surprised when it happens!

Our next retracement example is on a daily chart of Google stock (see Figure 3-7). Here we measured a swing from high to low looking for possible resistance. The retracement was from the 1/16/07 high of 513.00 to the 3/5/07 low at 437.00. A key high was made just a touch below the 0.382 retracement back to this high.

Looking more closely at this chart, you should notice that there are smaller swings within the larger swing that we measured. We can take these smaller swings and also run Fibonacci retracements that could end

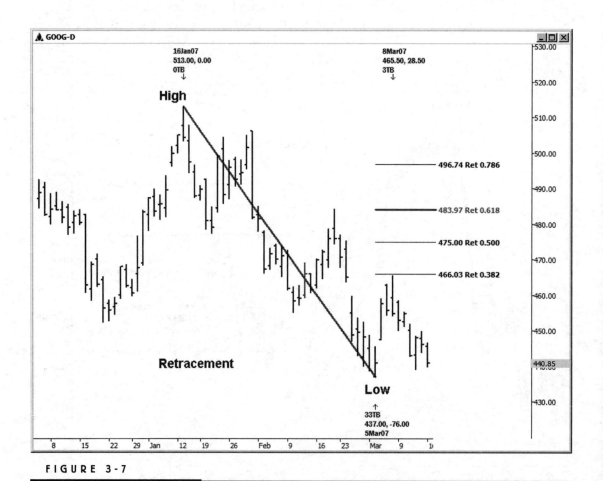

FIGURE 3-7

up overlapping the price retracements from the other swings. When levels start to overlap each other this way, this confluence indicates a more important price decision.

Let's look at another daily Google chart in Figure 3-8 and see how another retracement could be run from a swing within the larger swing that was retraced on the prior chart. This time we took the move from the 2/22/07 high at 484.24 to the 3/5/07 low made at 437.00. In this case, the 0.618 retracement at 466.19 produced a turn that just happened to overlap the 0.382 retracement at 466.03 from the prior chart. The actual high was made at 465.50—close enough for government work.

FIGURE 3-8

There were actually a couple of other price relationships that overlapped this area that you will learn about as you move forward in this book. With such a healthy confluence of price relationships that could be identified in advance, this work would have definitely warned the trader of an impending reversal to the downside from the 3/8/07 high!

Figure 3-9 is a retracement example in which we are looking at a daily FOREX chart of the British pound. Measuring from the 6/29/06 low to the 8/8/06 high looking for possible support, the only retracement that produced a change in trend was the 50 percent mark. This was not a perfect hit, but it was close enough to watch for reversal indications. Another important low was made above the 0.618 retracement. Though that was

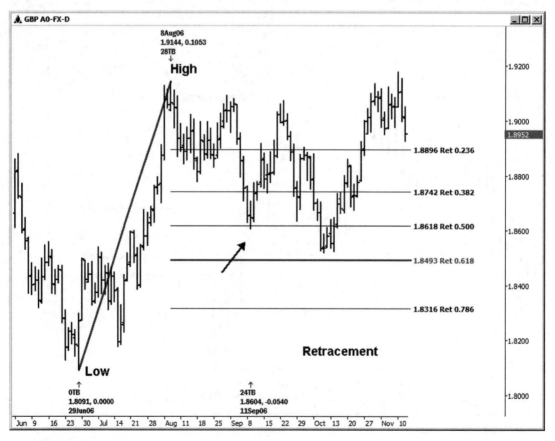

FIGURE 3-9

not really close enough to be considered a hit, it still doesn't hurt to be aware of this important retracement of a major swing.

In this next retracement example, Figure 3-10, we are looking at a General Motors daily chart and running the retracements from the 4/5/06 low to the 9/13/06 high, looking for possible support on the pullback. In this case, we saw only a minor pullback to the 0.236 retracement before the rally resumed in this stock.

FIGURE 3-10

This next retracement example is on a 15-minute E-mini Nasdaq futures chart (see Figure 3-11). We measured from the 1822.25 swing high to the 1789.00 swing low, looking for possible resistance on the way back up. On this chart, we saw only a decent reaction off the 0.618 retracement back to the high. The retracement came in at 1809.55. The actual high was made just a touch below this, at 1809.00.

FIGURE 3-11

Figure 3-12 is a daily chart for the 3M company. It shows where we retraced from the 7/25/06 low to the 9/19/06 high, looking for possible support. In this case, the stock pulled back to the 0.382 retracement, and then the rally resumed.

FIGURE 3-12

Let's look at another example of a retracement on a 15-minute chart of the E-mini Russell contract. In Figure 3-13, we measured from the 815.60 high to the 796.80 swing low to look for possible resistance on the way back up. In this case, we saw only a reaction at the 0.786 retracement. The price actually fell short of this level by 2 ticks, but that is close enough. A healthy decline followed this retracement high.

FIGURE 3-13

CORRECT RETRACEMENTS

One of the ways in which you are going to create Fibonacci price cluster setups is by running retracements on multiple swings on the chart you are analyzing. Over the years, I have watched my students make mistakes by using some of the wrong swings in their analysis. I'm hoping that the following examples will show you how to avoid the same kind of errors.

In Figure 3-14, we are looking at a daily chart of Home Depot. I have identified a number of swings that could be used for our analysis in terms of running possible support zones. When running retracements of low-to-high swings, you need to run them from the lows to the highest high on the chart. For example, in this chart, besides running them from the 10/20/06 low to the 1/3/07 high, you could also run the ratios from the higher lows to the 1/3/07 high. The other swings I would run would be from the 11/14/06 low to the 1/3/07 high, the 11/28/06 low to the 1/3/07 high, the 12/12/06 low to the 1/3/07 high, and the 12/26/06 low to the 1/3/07 high. All of these swings would have value in setting up possible

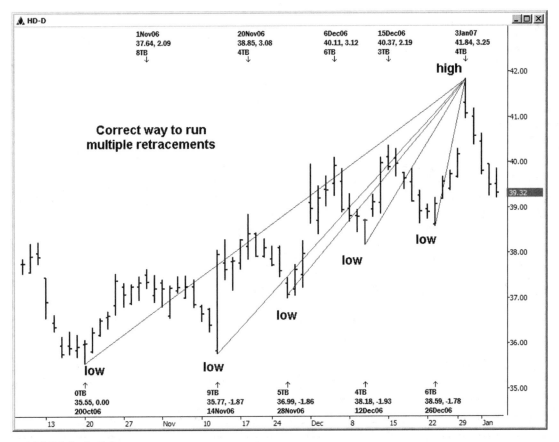

FIGURE 3-14

support as the market declined from the 1/3/07 high. When you run multiple price retracements, you will notice that some of these levels will overlap nicely. (This is what we want to see.)

INCORRECT RETRACEMENTS

In Figure 3-15, on this same chart of Home Depot, I am illustrating some of the swings that would *not* have value in defining possible support as we trade down from the 1/3/07 high. The swings illustrated may have had value for running possible support at *other* times, but they would not be relevant to the current market analysis. In other words, running a retracement from the 10/20/06 low to the 11/20/06 high would not be relevant

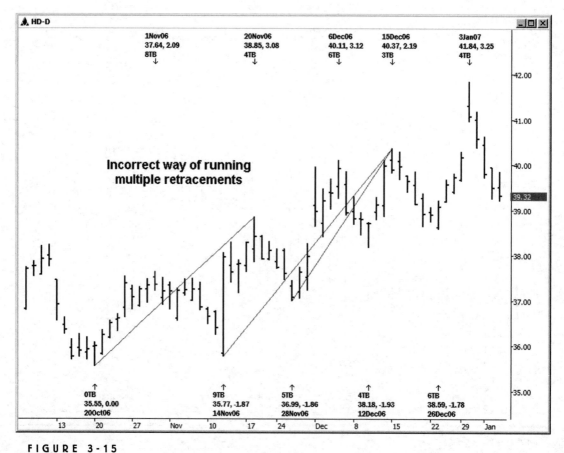

FIGURE 3-15

to the current market, where we are looking for support on a pullback from the 1/3/07 high. It would have been relevant when you were looking for support on a pullback from the 11/20/06 high. Once the 11/20/06 high was exceeded, however, you would have to use the new high at that time to run the possible support. Following that reasoning, using the 11/14/06 low to the 12/15/06 high or using the 11/28/06 low to the 12/15/06 high would not have been relevant to the current market analysis, although it would have been relevant before the 12/15/06 high was exceeded. I am hoping these visual examples are getting my point across.

CORRECT RETRACEMENTS HIGH TO LOW

Let's take a look at an example in the mini crude oil contract that shows the proper way to run multiple retracements for possible resistance from the 10/31/06 low. When retracing high-to-low swings, just remember to take all your highs and retrace from the lowest low, which in this case was the 10/31/06 low. You always want to use at least the distance from the highest high to the lowest low. Then, to add multiple retracements, use the distance from the lower highs to the lowest low. In Figure 3-16, you can see that all of the following swings were relevant to projecting possible resistance for the current market at that time.

7/17/06 high to 10/31/06 low
8/8/06 high to 10/31/06 low
8/25/06 high to 10/31/06 low
9/28/06 high to 10/31/06 low
10/17/06 high to 10/31/06 low

There is one more minor swing that could have been used in this case, but the high was only slightly lower than the 10/17/06 high. Since the highs are relatively close, it's almost redundant, although you can still choose to use it. Running all the retracements listed here would identify areas of possible resistance to the rally that started from the 10/31/06 swing low. If this low was violated, however, the retracements would have to be run all over again from the new lower low.

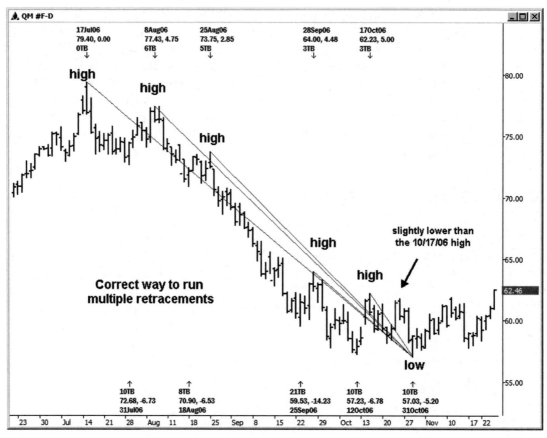

FIGURE 3-16

This second chart on the crude oil contract, Figure 3-17, illustrates some swings that would *not* have been relevant to the current market activity at that time because they were not being run from the lowest low made on 10/31/06. For example, running the retracement of the 7/17/06 high to the 9/25/06 low would have no value for the current analysis, since the 9/25/06 low had been exceeded. It would have had value when the 9/25/06 low was the lowest low, however. The other swings that would not have had value would be the 8/8/06 high to the 9/25/06 low and the 8/25/06 high to the 10/4/06 low, since the 10/31/06 low was the lowest low at the time of the analysis.

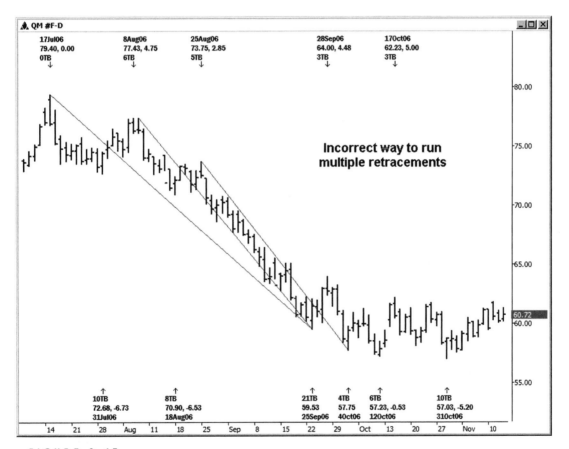

FIGURE 3-17

Before I move on to Fibonacci price extensions, I want to address a question that I am asked in almost all of my presentations. I'm always asked if old Fibonacci support levels become new resistance or if old resistance becomes new support. The answer is *no*; that is simply not part of the methodology. There are times where it will seem that this is the case, as a market will tend to pull back to a price zone after that zone is violated. The more accurate way to find new support and resistance levels, however, is to run the new levels that are created by the most recent price activity. We have to treat this market as a dynamic, living, and growing thing and continue to analyze it as such.

4 CHAPTER

FIBONACCI PRICE EXTENSIONS

In this chapter, I will show you multiple examples of Fibonacci price extensions, which are also run to set up possible support or resistance parameters for whatever market you are analyzing. Fibonacci price extensions are similar to price retracements, in that they are also run from prior lows to highs or from prior highs to lows, using only two data points to run the price relationships. The only difference is that with retracements, we are running the relationships of a prior swing that are less than 100 percent, or *retracing* the prior move, whereas with extensions, we are running the relationships of a prior swing that are *extending* beyond 100 percent of it. Even though you will more than likely be using the same price tool from your trading analysis program, these techniques are named differently to indicate whether the price relationship is occurring within the prior swing or extending beyond it.

Extensions are run from prior low-to-high swings using the ratios 1.272 and 1.618 for potential support. They are run from prior high-to-low swings using the ratios 1.272 and 1.618 for potential resistance. You may also add the ratios 2.618 and 4.236. I will use 2.618 as the third target for a trade setup, but I will look at 4.236 only if I am looking at a very extended move in a market and trying to look for a place where it might finally terminate.

I used the same Dynamic Trader tool shown in the retracement chapter to run the following price extension examples. Most analysis programs will run extensions from the same program tool, since they are also measured using only two price points on the chart. The math is the same, with the only difference being that retracements are defined as less than 100 percent of a prior swing and extensions are defined as beyond 100 percent of a prior swing.

Note: What I call price extensions in my work are labeled EX Ret on the Dynamic Trader charts that you will see in the following examples. Robert Miner, my mentor, refers to these as external price retracements rather than price extensions.

Our first price extension example is illustrated on a daily Russell cash index chart (see Figure 4-1). The 1.272 and 1.618 extensions were run from the 4/21/06 high to the 4/27/06 low for possible resistance to the rally that started with the 4/27/06 low. In this case, knowing where the 1.272

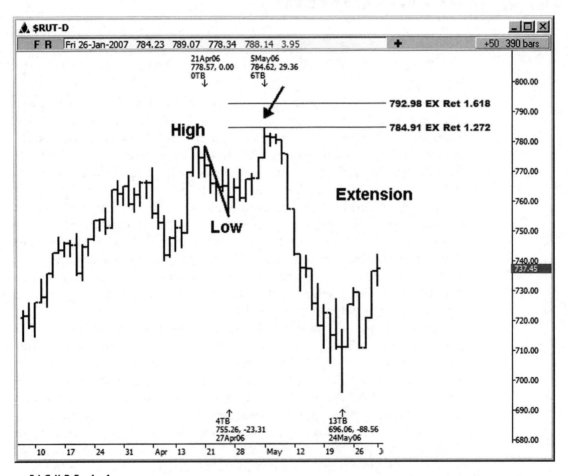

FIGURE 4-1

extension was would have been extremely valuable to a trader, as a very healthy decline followed a test of this resistance.

This next price extension example is illustrated on a 60-minute crude oil futures chart (see Figure 4-2). Here we measured from the low made at 51.58 on January 12, 2007, to the January 15, 2007, high made at 53.38 and ran the 1.272 and 1.618 extensions for possible support. Note that an important low was made within ticks of the 1.618 extension, where a rally of over 2.00 was seen! One thing I have learned by using price extensions over the years is that many moves tend to terminate—*if only temporarily*—at these extensions.

FIGURE 4-2

Let's look at another price extension example, this time on the mini-sized Dow. In Figure 4-3, we ran the high-to-low swing on this 15-minute chart to look for possible resistance on the way up. Notice that there was a minor decline off the 1.272 extension and then another minor decline off the 1.618 extension. The contract eventually rallied beyond both of these levels. This was not that unusual, since we were in a healthy uptrend, but these levels did offer some temporary resistance to the move, which is why as a trader you want to be aware of them.

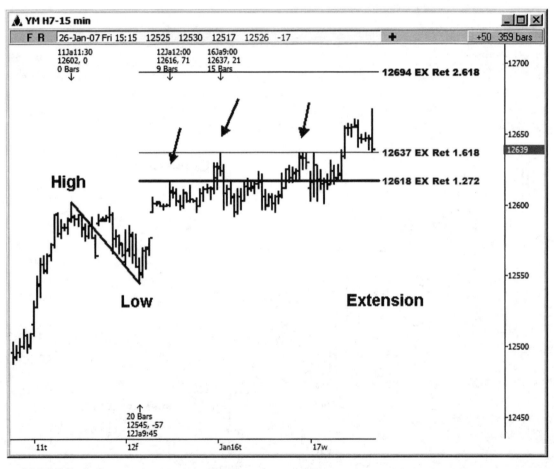

FIGURE 4-3

The next extension example is on a 15-minute E-mini S&P contract (see Figure 4-4). We measured from the high made at 1435.75 to the low at 1429.25, looking for possible resistance on the way up. The S&P barely paused at the 1.272 extension, but did pause and show us a minor decline at the 1.618 extension. Again none of this was too surprising, since the 15-minute chart was showing a healthy bullish pattern.

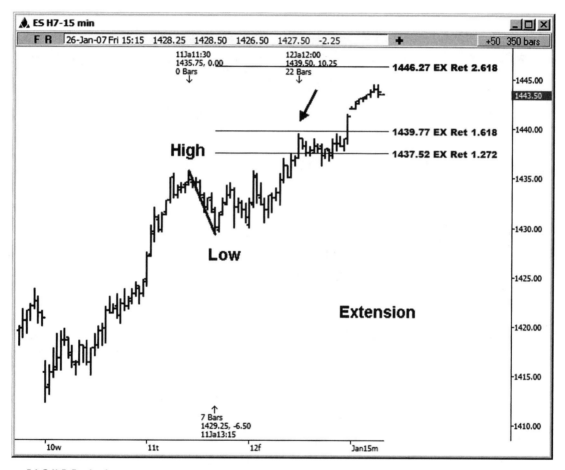

FIGURE 4-4

Figure 4-5 is another example of an extension that was run on a 15-minute chart of the E-mini S&P contract. We measured a prior low-to-high swing (from the 1/17/2007 low of 1435.50, made at 2:15 p.m. central time, to the 1/18/2007 high of 1440.75, made at 9:00 a.m. central time) and ran the 1.272 and 1.618 price extensions for potential support. The S&P contract did not even pause at the 1.272 extension; however, a tradable low was made at the 1.618 extension of the same swing.

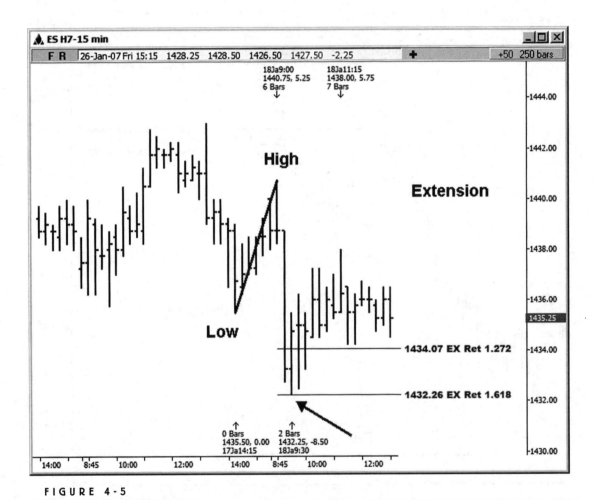

FIGURE 4-5

The next example of a price extension (see Figure 4-6) is made on the daily chart of the E-mini Russell contract. The 1.618 extension of the 12/05/06 high to the 1/9/07 low came in at 832.10 after the 1.272 extension was easily surpassed. One of the features on the Dynamic Trader software is that the program will automatically delete the price relationships that have been surpassed by a decent margin. In this case, this is why the 1.272 extension is not illustrated on the chart. The actual high was made at 831.90, just 2 ticks below this extension. A 58.70-point decline has followed this extension so far. I continually remind my traders to tighten up stops on their positions when we get near the 1.272 price extension of a prior swing or beyond it, since many moves terminate at least temporarily around extensions.

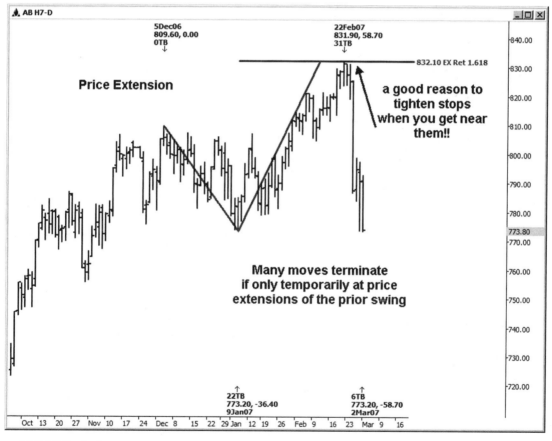

FIGURE 4-6

In Figure 4-7, we are looking at an extension on a daily chart of SBUX. Here, we measured from the 12/1/06 low made at 34.90 to the 12/5/06 high made at 37.14, looking for possible support. We did see a nice bounce around the 1.272 extension of this swing, although it was not a perfect hit. The low made on 1/26/07, however, was made within ticks of the 1.618 extension at 33.52. The actual low was made at 33.49.

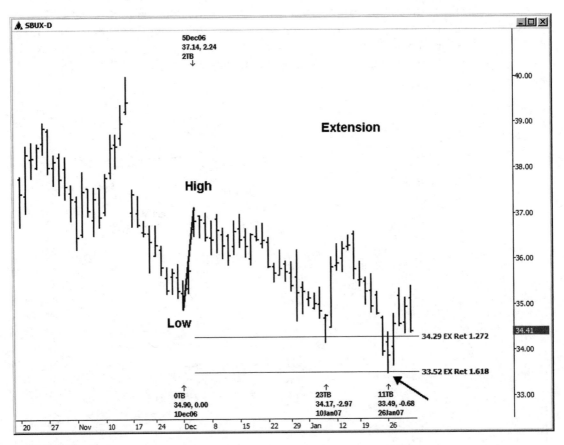

FIGURE 4-7

On the daily chart of IBM shown in Figure 4-8, we measured from the 11/29/05 high at 89.94 to the 7/18/06 low at 72.73, looking for possible resistance to the rally from the 7/18/06 low. In this case, the 1.618 extension provided such resistance. Again note that this was not a *perfect* hit: the extension came in at 100.58, and the actual high was made at 100.90. However, as long as a level is not taken out by a huge margin, I will typically leave it up on the chart and still watch for a possible reaction around it.

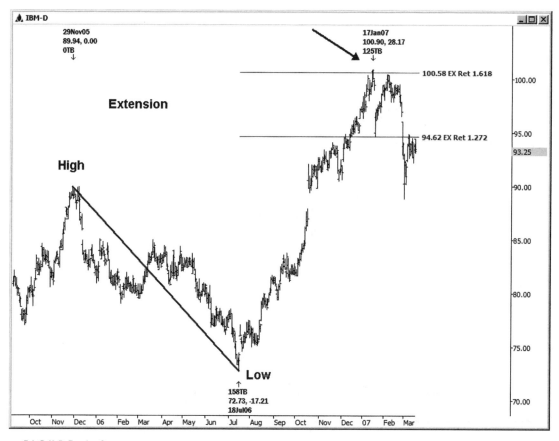

FIGURE 4-8

Google is a stock that seems to respect market geometry more often than not. In Figure 4-9, we measured from the 2/12/07 low made at 455.02 to the 2/22/07 high made at 484.24, looking for possible support at the price extensions. This stock barely stalled at the 1.272 extension, although we saw a tradable bounce after testing the area of the 1.618 extension.

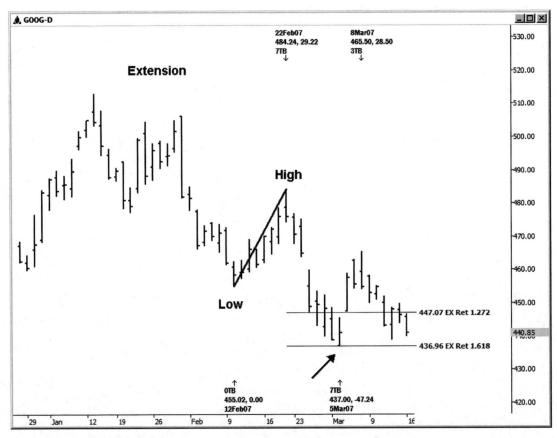

FIGURE 4-9

In Figure 4-10, we ran the extensions on a daily chart of Intel, using the move from the 10/16/06 high at 22.03 to the 11/6/06 low at 20.32, looking for possible resistance. The 1.272 extension was hit and held exactly at the 22.50 level. A healthy decline followed this high.

F I G U R E   4 - 1 0

On the daily chart of Home Depot in Figure 4-11, we ran the extensions of the move from the 11/1/06 high at 37.64 to the 11/14/06 low at 35.77, looking for possible resistance. In this case, the 1.618 extension produced a tradable high. This stock then resumed the uptrend after a healthy pullback from the 11/20/06 high. Keep in mind that many of these Fibonacci price relationships will *not* produce a change in trend and are violated every day. In later chapters I will show you examples where even a cluster of these price relationships fails to produce even a minor change in trend. This work is not magic, but if you learn how to use it properly, it *will* definitely provide you with a trading edge.

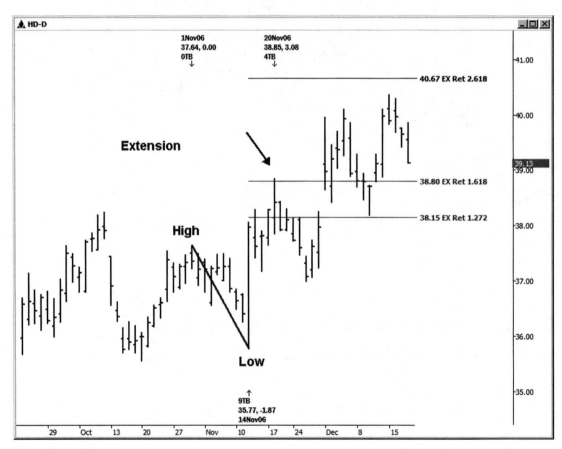

FIGURE 4-11

In the daily chart of Yahoo shown in Figure 4-12, we ran the extensions of the move from the 6/7/05 high at 38.95 to the 9/21/05 low at 31.60, which included multiple swings within this larger swing. We were looking for possible resistance at the 1.272 and 1.618 extensions on this chart. A tradable high was made just a few cents below the 1.618 extension at 43.49.

FIGURE 4-12

FIGURE 4-13

Fibonacci price relationships can be used on any time frame chart. Figure 4-13 is a three-minute chart of the E-mini S&P. Measuring from the 1398.50 low to the 1403.50 high, we would be looking for possible support at the extension of this swing. A tradable low was made off the 1.618 extension in this case.

Author Tip In my chat room, I use the auto-typer feature to remind my traders constantly that many moves terminate at extensions, since I see this occur so often.

This daily cash S&P chart (see Figure 4-14) is yet another example of the market turning on a dime when either the 1.272 or the 1.618 extension has been met. Taking the move from the 3/5/07 low to the 3/9/07 high, the 1.272 extension of that swing came in at 1364.13. The actual low was made at 1363.98. A dramatic 74-point rally has followed this low so far.

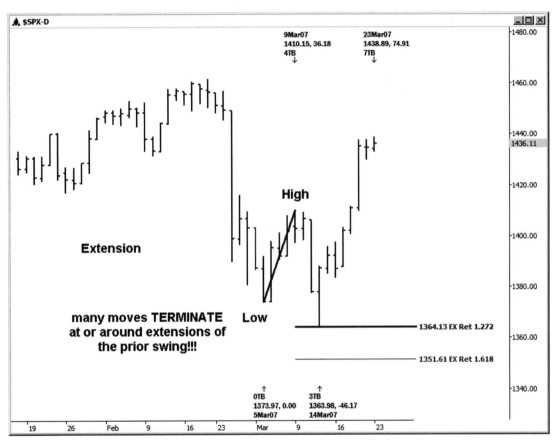

FIGURE 4-14

In this chapter, the chart examples have illustrated that many moves tend to terminate at the extensions of prior swings. These levels are well worth knowing as a trader. When you project them in advance, you have the advantage of knowing that the odds that the market move will terminate are higher than usual. Now it's time to look at Fibonacci price projections in our next chapter.

5

C H A P T E R

FIBONACCI PRICE PROJECTIONS OR OBJECTIVES

Last but not least, in this chapter I will show you how to apply Fibonacci price *projections* to the chart we are analyzing. These projections are sometimes also called price *objectives*. I tend to indicate them on my charts by the letters PO for price objectives rather than projections.

These price projections are run from three data points and are comparing swings in the same direction. They are run from a prior low-to-high swing and then projected from another low for possible resistance, *or* they are run from a prior high-to-low swing and projected from another high for possible support. Here we use 1.00 and 1.618 ratios to run the projections.

The 100 percent projection is also where we find *symmetry*. (This concept will be discussed at length in the chapter on symmetry trade setups.) What you need to know at this point is that symmetry is defined as similarity or equality of swings in the same direction. I use symmetry projections every day for setting up trades in the direction of the trend. This concept will become crystal clear as we walk through the chart examples.

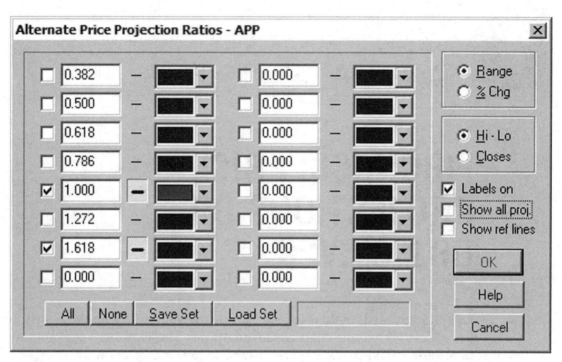

FIGURE 5-1

Price Projection Tool on Dynamic Trader

To run these price relationships, you have to use an analysis tool that allows the use of three points on the chart. In the Dynamic Trader software, it is called the *alternate price projection tool*. The setup of this tool is illustrated in Figure 5-1.

There can be some confusion when I teach how to run the price projection relationships, since many technical analysis programs call the Fibonacci tool using three points an *extension* tool rather than a projection tool. Just remember that to run your projections to compare swings in the same direction, you need to use the tool that allows you to choose three points, regardless of what it is called.

Note: What I call price projections or objectives in my work will be labeled in the following Dynamic Trader chart examples as APPs or Alternate Price Projections.

Our first projection example is Figure 5-2, a daily stock chart of General Motors. Remember that with the projection tool that uses three points, we are comparing swings in the same direction. Here we measured the swing from A to B, which was a 3.90 swing. We then projected both the 1.0 and 1.618 projections of the first swing from point C, looking for potential resistance. The 1.0 projection came in at 34.28. There was no reaction at this first projection. The 1.618 projection came in at 36.69. Notice that the rally in GM terminated just below this second resistance projection—at least temporarily.

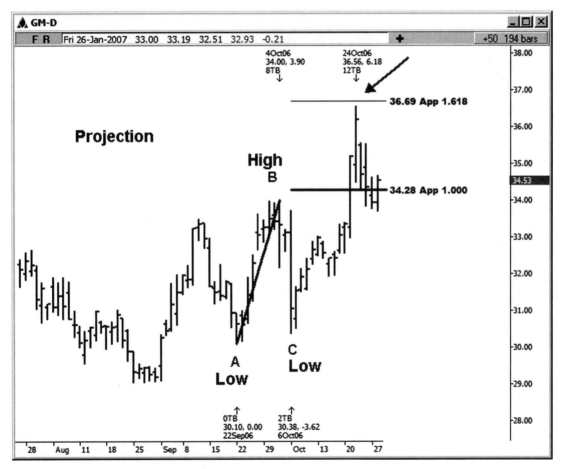

FIGURE 5-2

Our second projection example is on a three-minute chart of the E-mini S&P contract. In Figure 5-3, we are using only the 1.0 projection, since we are comparing *corrective rallies* within a downtrend. I like to compare corrective swings because more often than not, you will find similarity or equality in these swings. This becomes a powerful tool to aid in our entries in the direction of the trend.

Notice that the first swing illustrated on this chart was 2.50 E-mini S&P points from the 1434.25 swing low to the 1436.75 swing high. We then took 100 percent of this swing and projected it from the low made at 1433.75, which gave us the 1436.25 level for the projection and possible resistance.

The actual high was made exactly at the 100 percent projection. A decline of more than 4.00 points was seen from this *symmetry projection*. In this case there was perfect symmetry (equality), as both swings were exactly 2.50 points.

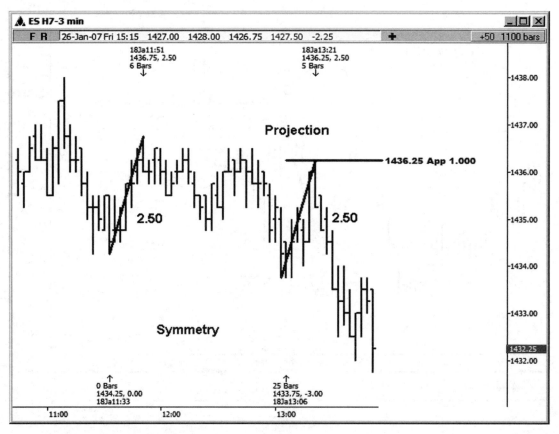

FIGURE 5-3

Let's look at another price projection example in Google stock. In Figure 5-4, we measured the swing from point A to point B and then ran our projections of 1.0 and 1.618 from point C, looking for possible resistance. The 1.0 projection came in at 389.32. Though it was not a perfect hit in price (the actual high was made at 390.00), it definitely ended up producing a nice downside reversal. The 1.618 projection at 402.50 didn't provide any resistance at all in this case.

There will be days when some of these Fibonacci price relationships will hit exactly at the level projected, and it will seem very magical. Don't expect to always see perfection with this work, however. As long as a level

FIGURE 5-4

is not violated by a huge margin or does not fall short of a level by a huge margin, it still has value as a price decision. Personally, I have been found guilty of erasing Fibonacci levels too quickly. My chat room traders are the first ones to call this to my attention.

Figure 5-5 is a daily chart of Intel stock. Here we measured the swing from point A to point B, which was a 2.55 decline. We then projected 1.0 of this decline from point C, for a projection of possible support at 19.95. The actual low in this case was made at 20.03, which was just a bit short of the support level. There was definitely some similarity (symmetry) between these swings, as the first swing was a decline of 2.55 and the second was a decline of 2.47.

FIGURE 5-5

Let's look at another example of a price projection in the mini-sized Dow. On this 15-minute chart (Figure 5-6), we started with a rally from point A to point B that was 32 points. We then multiplied the range of this first swing by 1.0 and 1.618 (actually, the computer program did) and projected the results from point C. In this case, all we saw was a short-term stall around the 1.0 projection. Beyond that, the projections really didn't provide much resistance to the rally. (Remember that many of these price relationships will be violated and won't have any predictive value at all!)

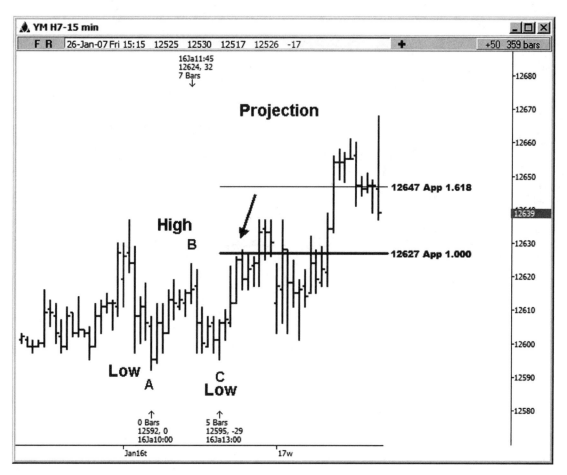

FIGURE 5-6

Again, I don't want to give you the idea that Fibonacci price relationships always hold, so I'd like to share an example in Google where the price projections did not produce any change at all (see Figure 5-7). It would be irresponsible of me as an author to show you *only* examples where the levels have held. Besides the fact that there is no methodology or analysis in existence that will work 100 percent of the time, as a trader you would know *not* to enter a trade against these price zones if you do not see any reversal indications or entry triggers as they are tested.

FIGURE 5-7

Figure 5-8 is an example of a price projection on a daily cash chart of the Russell index. We measured from the 2/14/06 low (point A) to the 3/3/06 high (point B) and ran the projections from the 3/8/06 low (point C) for possible resistance. Notice the minor reaction at the area of the 1.0 projection and then the healthier decline just a touch below the 1.618 projection of this same swing.

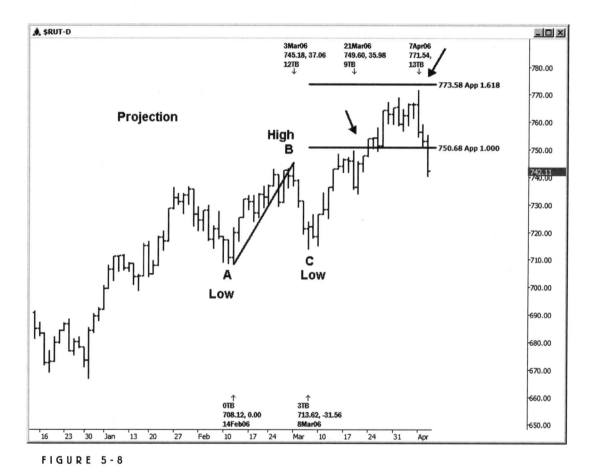

FIGURE 5-8

In the S&P cash daily chart (see Figure 5-9), we measured from the 8/13/04 low at 1060.72 (point A) to the 10/6/04 high at 1142.05 (point B) and then projected the ratios from the 10/25/04 low at 1090.19 (point C), looking for possible resistance. In this example, we saw a minor stall at the 1.0 projection of this swing from A to B. In addition, we saw a much healthier downside reversal a bit below the 1.618 projection.

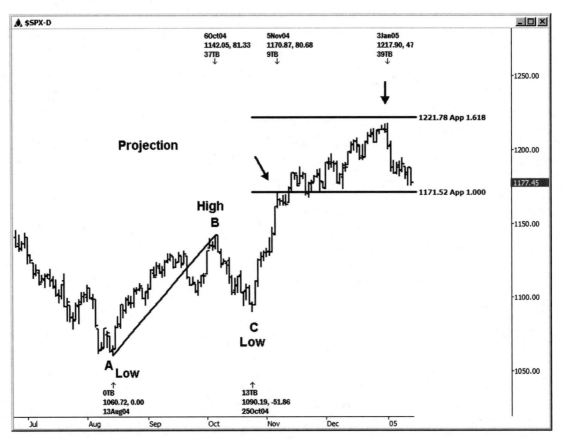

FIGURE 5-9

In the next example, in the daily cash S&P chart, Figure 5-10, we measured from the 1/8/07 low at 1403.97 (point A) to the 1/25/07 high at 1440.69 (point B) and then projected the ratios from the 1/26/07 low at 1416.96 (point C), looking for possible resistance. A tradable high was seen just a touch below the 1.0 projection. (We did not test the 1.618 in this case.)

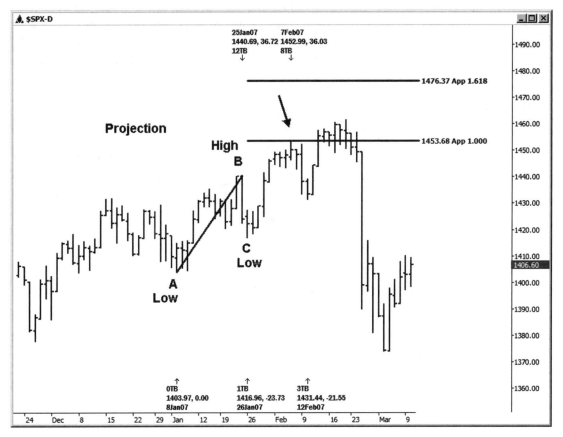

FIGURE 5-10

Our next example is in the FOREX market—the Canadian dollar (see Figure 5-11). Since we are looking at a healthy uptrend in this case, we wanted to use the projection tool to look for possible symmetry support within the uptrend. When we took the move from the high made on 12/18/06 to the low made on 12/20/06 and then projected from the new high made on 1/11/07, the 1.0 projection from the 1/11/07 high showed us possible support at the 1.1644 area. The actual low was made at 1.1646, which was a couple of pips short of the projection. This low was followed by a beautiful rally to 1.1851, which was a 205-pip rally from the 1/16/07 low. Notice that this rally made it up to the 1.272 extension and then stalled.

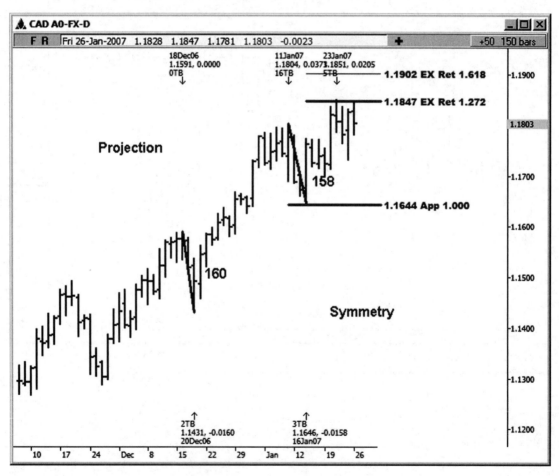

FIGURE 5-11

56

Next, let's take a look at JC Penney stock on a daily chart (Figure 5-12). Here, we measured the range from the 11/13/06 high to the 12/1/06 low (points A and B) and projected from the 12/15/06 high (point C) for possible support. In this case, the 1.0 projection of that prior swing pretty much caught the low before a rally of 11.95. (The 1.618 projection was not tested.)

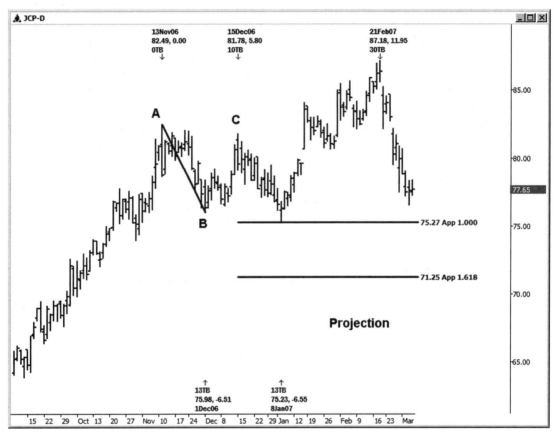

FIGURE 5-12

On the next daily stock chart of YHOO, it may be a bit difficult to see an obvious place to run a projection (see Figure 5-13). The swing low at point C is not as well defined as some of the other examples you've seen so far. Running Fibonacci price relationships on a chart is sometimes more of an art than a science. There will be times when you just have to use some common sense and/or intuition while doing your analysis. Even though the swings in this example may not be obvious on a daily chart, if you took this down to a 60-minute chart, they would be more obvious. You can always go down to a lower time frame chart and make an assessment if you are wondering whether or not to use a certain high or low in your calculations.

We measured the swing from the 10/25/05 low to the 11/1/05 high (points A and B) and then ran the projections from the 11/3/05 low (point C), looking for possible resistance. We did not see any reaction at the 1.0 projection of the prior swing, although we did see a tradable high develop right around the 1.618 projection of this same prior swing.

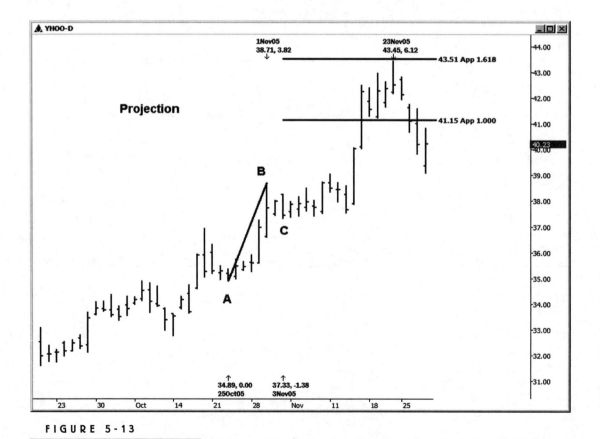

FIGURE 5-13

Figure 5-14 shows the daily GM chart where we measured from the 6/8/06 low to the 6/30/06 high (points A and B) and then ran the projections from the 7/14/06 low (point C), looking for possible resistance. On this chart, we saw a nice reaction off the 1.0 projection of that prior swing. (While the reaction just below the 1.618 projection was not really close enough for this perfectionist to call it a hit, it is still a good habit to trail stops up closer to the current market activity any time you are moving close to an important price decision. Strategies using trailing stop-loss orders will be discussed later in this book.)

FIGURE 5-14

The last several chapters showed examples of how you can run the three different types of Fibonacci price relationships that we will use to create our trade setups: price retracements, price extensions, and price projections. The next chapter will look at the "price clustering effect," or "confluence," of these price relationships, which will identify our first type of trade setup: a Fibonacci price cluster.

6
CHAPTER

FIBONACCI PRICE CLUSTER SETUPS: TRADE SETUP 1

My definition of a price cluster is the coincidence of at least three Fibonacci price relationships that come together within a relatively tight range. These price clusters identify key support and resistance zones that can be considered to be trade setups. A price cluster can be created from three retracements, three extensions, three projections, or the combination of any of these price relationships.

A price cluster can also develop with a coincidence of more than three price relationships. Three is just the minimum number required to meet the definition. You may see five to ten price relationships come together in a relatively tight range. When you do see more of these price relationships come together, this doesn't mean that the zone is more likely to hold, but it does tell you that it is a very important price decision zone. If the zone holds, you are likely to see a nice move off of it a high percentage of the time. If the same key zone is violated, don't be surprised if you start to see an acceleration of the original trend going into the zone. There are times when I see these large clusters develop not too far from current market activity, and they tend to act like a magnet for price.

TRENDS

When I'm setting up price clusters in the market, as far as trade *entries* are concerned, I want to focus on the clusters that set up in the direction of the trend on the chart we are analyzing. These will be the higher-probability setups. The simple definition of a trend that I use is one that involves looking at the pattern on the chart. Are we looking at an *uptrend*, with a general pattern of higher highs and higher lows, or are we looking at a *downtrend*, with a general pattern of lower lows and lower highs?

I believe in going with the flow rather than attempting to swim upstream, as many traders do with countertrend trades. If I'm looking at a bullish chart pattern (higher highs and higher lows), I set up my clusters for possible entries on the buy side, in keeping with the trend. If I'm looking at a bearish chart pattern (lower lows and lower highs), I look at the clusters for entries on the sell side to help me enter in the direction of the downtrend. I look for the clusters that show up "counter" to the trend in order to help manage profits and exit strategies. For example, if we are long and we are seeing a resistance cluster within an uptrend, I will suggest that my traders tighten up stops and/or take partial profits.

A price cluster that is counter to the immediate trend is still considered a trade setup, although you need to be aware that the odds that one of these clusters will turn into a winning trade are *lower* than those on the clusters that are not fighting the trend. Using proper trade filters and triggers when these countertrend setups develop will improve your odds in this case.

Diagram of Uptrend/General Pattern of Higher Highs and Lows—Focus on Setting Up Buy Clusters

Figure 6-1 is a daily cash S&P chart. The general pattern of this market is up from the July 2006 low to the February 2007 high. What I mean by *general* is that the chart mostly shows a pattern of higher highs and higher lows. However, there are places on this chart where you have taken out a prior swing low, even though the overall direction of the market is still trending upward. Another way to look at this is through the eyes of a four-year-old. Have a four-year-old look at a chart for you, then ask the child if prices are going higher or lower. The child will typically step back, observe, and give you the correct answer by observing the forest and not the trees.

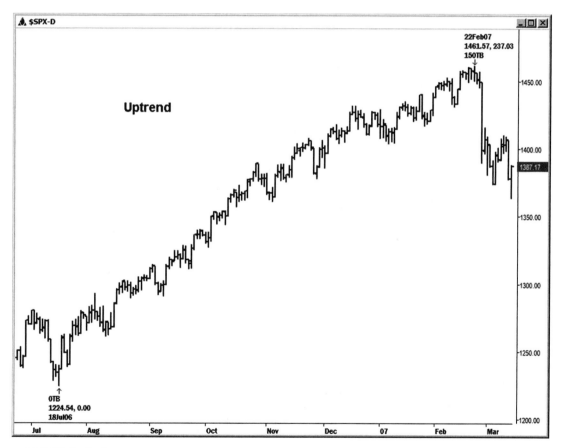

FIGURE 6-1

Diagram of Downtrend/General Pattern of Lower Lows and Highs—Focus on Setting Up Sell Clusters

Figure 6-2 is a daily cash S&P chart. The general pattern of this market is down from the May 2001 high to the September 2001 low. What I mean by *general* is that the chart mostly shows a pattern of lower lows and lower highs. However, there are places on this chart where you have taken out a prior swing high, even though the overall direction of the market was still trending downward. Remember to look at the chart with the mind of a four-year-old!

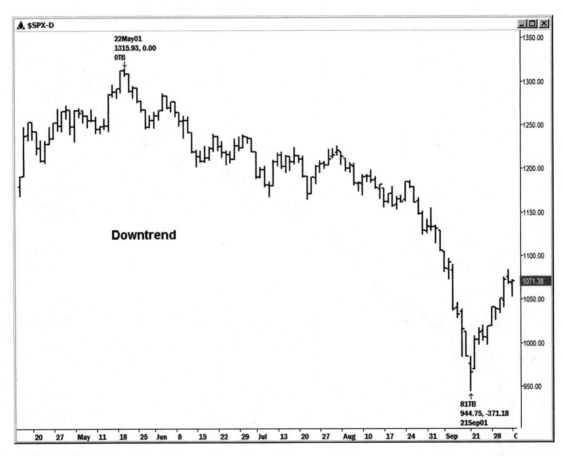

FIGURE 6-2

MONEY MANAGEMENT

Before I get into the examples of the actual cluster setups, let's go over how you should generally be thinking of using them to profit in the market. First, let's look at defining your risk. When you enter a market using a price cluster setup, the *maximum risk* is defined as a few ticks above or below the *extreme* of the price cluster zone. There are a couple of other ways you can place stop-loss orders with a lot less risk than the maximum. (Additional strategies will be discussed later.)

Next, you should have a general idea of what the profit potential for the trade is. My minimum trade target for any price cluster setup is always the 1.272 extension of the swing into the cluster zone. This target is met a high percentage of the time, especially in a nicely trending market, but keep in mind that it is not *always* met. My second target from this same swing is always 1.618, and then my third target is 2.618.

There are a few things that I need to point out about trade targets. Since the target for a setup is not *always* met, make sure you use good money management. This means either moving a stop to breakeven or trailing one as the trade moves in your favor. This way if you don't attain the 1.272 target, you are protecting yourself from a loss. Also note that the 1.272 target is often surpassed. This is a reason for keeping at least a partial position beyond your first target. Instead, you can use a trailing stop on the balance of your position and let the market take you out when the move loses momentum, rather than trying to determine in advance how far the market will go and how much it wants to give you on a trade.

PRICE CLUSTER EXAMPLES

Now let's go through some price cluster setup examples. To help you follow along with these examples, I will reference either the dates or the prices of the prior highs and lows I am using to run the price relationships.

In the first example of a price cluster setup, I will walk you through each step, starting with looking at a blank chart and deciding which side of the market to set it up on. In the later examples, I will still illustrate where the price cluster relationships are being projected from, but with fewer charts than in the first example.

Let's look at a blank E-mini Dow chart to decide which side of the market we want to set up. Here we are looking at a 30-minute chart of the June 2007 contract (see Figure 6-3). To me, the pattern is clearly defined as bullish by the general pattern of higher highs and higher lows. Since I want to focus on setting up my clusters in the direction of the trend of the chart I am analyzing, I want to set up all possible price support relationships in this case. Then I will look for a confluence or clustering of price relationships that will define my trade setup.

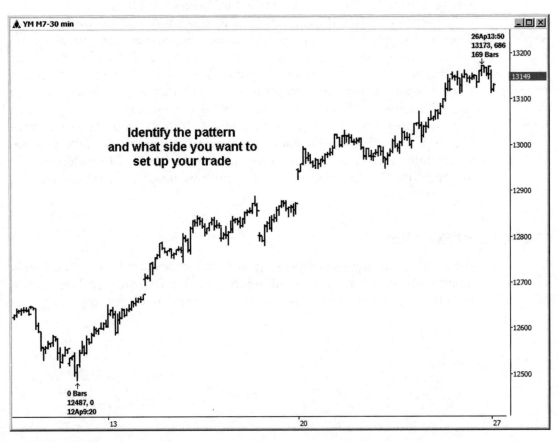

FIGURE 6-3

There were two obvious swings on which to run the Fibonacci price retracements: the 12781 low to the 13173 high and the 12948 low to the 13173 high (see Figure 6-4). You can see where some of these possible support levels came in. (Don't worry if you don't understand why I chose those swings just yet. By the time you go through all the examples in this book, you should have a better idea of how to choose the swings for this analysis.)

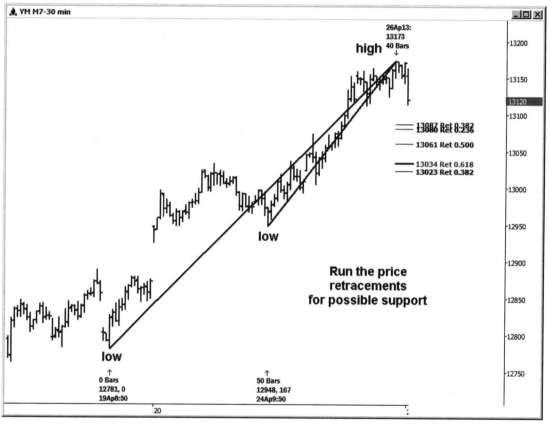

FIGURE 6-4

Once I run the retracements, I look and see whether running any price extensions of the prior swings for possible support makes any sense. In this example, I ran the extensions from the 13112 low to the 13173 high and also the extensions from the 13124 low to the 13173 high. The 1.272 and 1.618 extensions of those swings are illustrated in Figure 6-5.

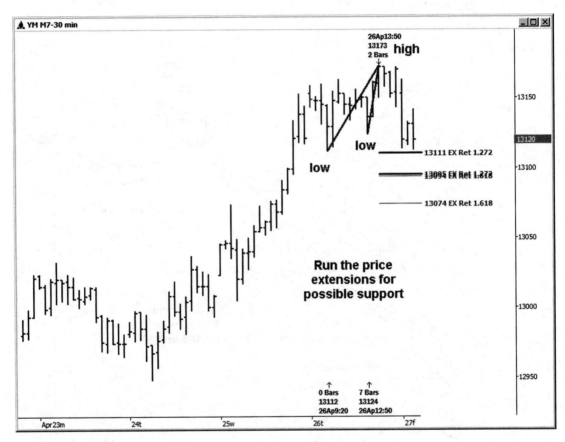

FIGURE 6-5

Last but not least, I need to determine what projections I can run for possible support. In this case, I see that I want to run only the symmetry or 1.0 projections of the prior declines in this bullish swing, since the 4/12/07 low was made at 12487. I'm running only these 1.0 projections rather than the 1.618 ratio as well, since I only want to compare the prior corrective declines with any new decline. In Figure 6-6, I have labeled the prior declines that I am going to measure and project from the 13173 high. The results of these projections are illustrated on the chart.

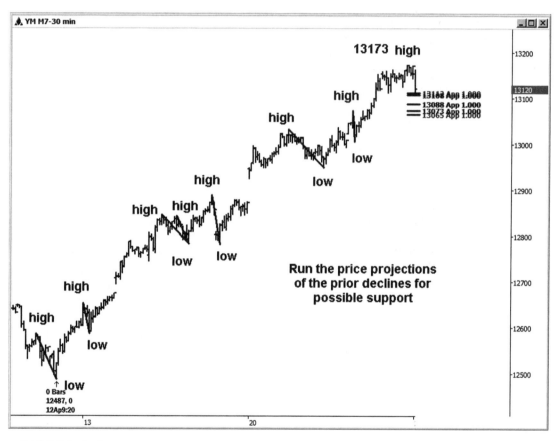

FIGURE 6-6

Author Tip The process of running these Fibonacci price relationships does *not* have to be done in a specific order. You can run the projections or the extensions first if you like. What is more important is that you run them all and then look for the clustering effect.

Figure 6-7 illustrates all the price relationships in this Dow example coming together. Let's focus on the first two areas on this chart that are clustering nicely. First, we have a key price cluster decision/trade setup at the 13107–13112 area. Second, we have a key price cluster decision/trade setup at the 13087–13095 area. I will start to get interested in the other zones only if we start violating these first key decisions.

FIGURE 6-7

Figure 6-8 illustrates the results of the analysis. This trade was actually set up in my chat room on 4/27/07. A low was made at 13113, which was just a tick above the high end of the first price cluster zone. A 75-point rally from this price cluster low was eventually seen. The dollar value of this run was $375.00 per contract, although a trader would expect to catch only some of the move in the middle between the cluster low and where the rally terminated.

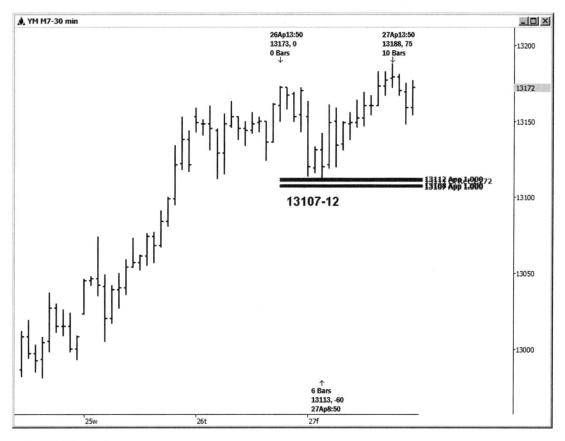

FIGURE 6-8

Since the high end of the cluster zone is what held, I am going to show you the exact price relationships that came together between 13107 and 13112, starting with the price projections that are illustrated in Figure 6-9.

1.0 projection from the 12653 high to the 12587 low, projected from the 13173 high = 13107 (point 1 to point 2 from point 7)

1.0 projection from the 12847 high to the 12782 low, projected from the 13173 high = 13108 (point 3 to point 5 from point 7)

1.0 projection from the 12843 high to the 12782 low, projected from the 13173 high = 13112 (point 4 to point 5 from point 7)

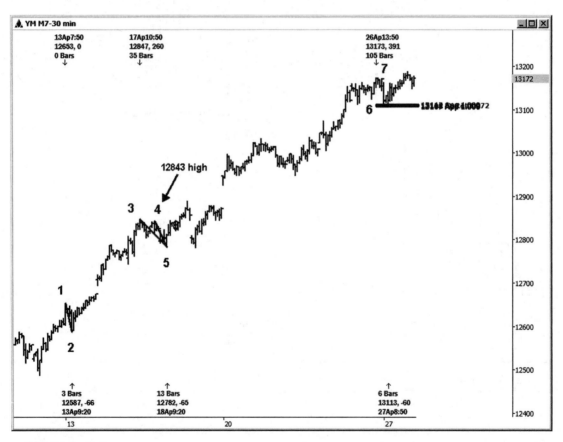

FIGURE 6-9

Figure 6-10 illustrates the price extension that overlapped the prior symmetry projections.

1.272 extension of the 13124 low to the 13173 high = 13111
(point 6 to point 7)

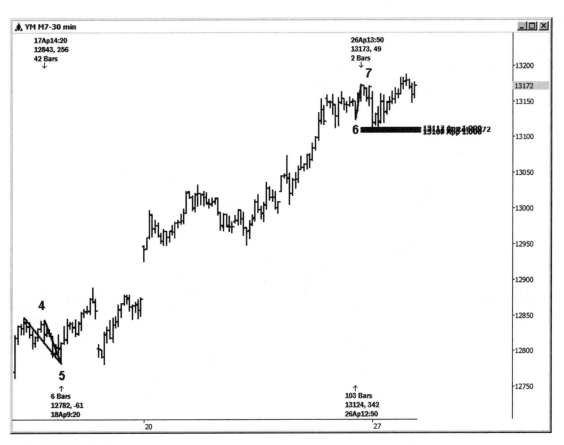

FIGURE 6-10

73

Next let's look at another example on the mini-sized Dow, this time on a 15-minute chart. The general pattern in Figure 6-11 was bearish, which is why I focused on setting up the sell side in this example. An important price cluster high was made at 12622. Let's go through the actual swings and the creation of the cluster, and see how you could have used this information to your advantage.

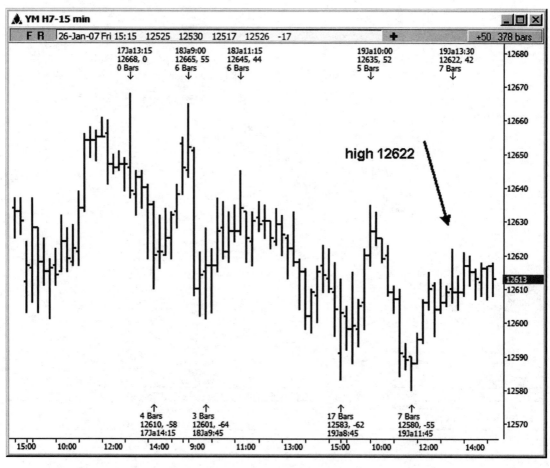

FIGURE 6-11

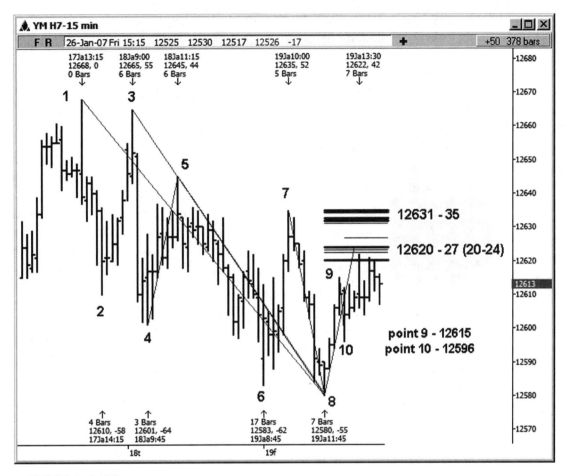

FIGURE 6-12

A healthy cluster of price relationships came in at the 12620–12627 area in this example. Figure 6-12 shows the individual price relationships that defined this cluster. In this example, I have numbered the key swing highs and lows for you to follow along with the analysis.

.50 retracement of the 12668 high to the 12580 low = 12624
   (point 1 to point 8)

.50 retracement of the 12665 high to the 12580 low = 12623
   (point 3 to point 8)

.618 retracement of the 12645 high to the 12580 low = 12620 (point 5 to point 8)

.786 retracement of the 12635 high to the 12580 low = 12623 (point 7 to point 8)

1.0 projection of the 12601 low to the 12645 high, projected from the 12580 low = 12624 (point 4 to point 5 projected from point 8)

1.272 extension of the 12615 high to the 12596 low = 12620 (point 9 to point 10)

1.618 extension of the 12615 high to the 12596 low = 12627 (point 9 to point 10)

Note that the swing from point 9 to point 10 was minor compared with most of the swings used for this analysis. If you are just learning this type of work, it may be difficult to identify that swing. I've been doing this work long enough, however, to know that this swing, which would be more obvious on a five-minute chart, would be a good confirming ratio for this cluster zone.

On this particular chart, I also left the projections for another cluster that developed right above our initial example at the 12631–12635 area. It is not unusual for more than one cluster zone to develop on the chart you are analyzing. In most of my book examples, however, I will erase the other price relationships so that we can focus on one setup at a time.

This price cluster setup was one of the *higher-probability setups*, since it was set up in the direction of the trend of this 15-minute chart which was down. With the standout resistance identified at the 12620–12627 area, as long as the market did not violate this resistance by any meaningful margin, you would look at taking any sell triggers that coordinate with this trade setup (see Figure 6-13). The initial decline from the high made at 12622 lasted 119 points. It looks like it would have taken a while to trigger an entry, but if you were patient and used good money management skills, it would have been worth quite a bit of cash.

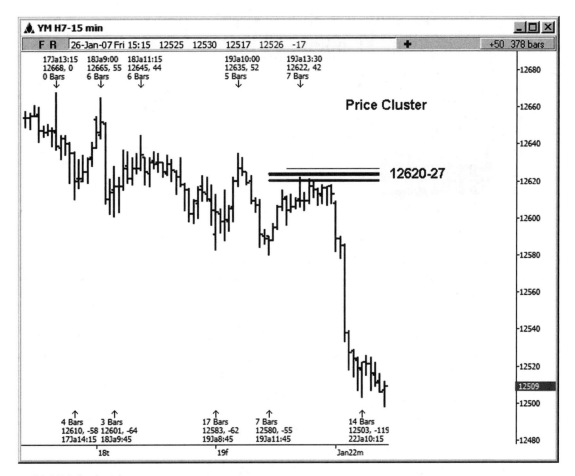

FIGURE 6-13

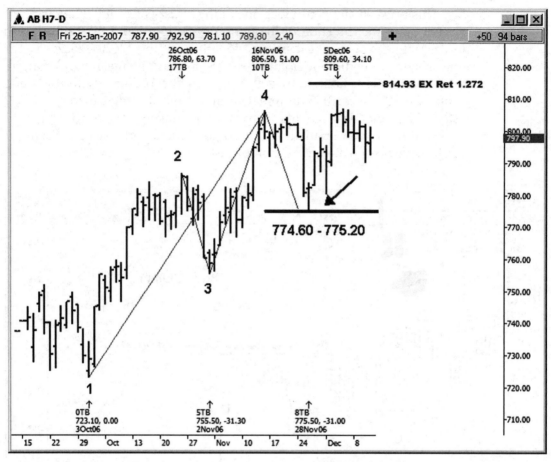

FIGURE 6-14

Our next example is on the E-mini Russell contract, the March 2007 daily chart (see Figure 6-14). This price cluster came in between 774.60 and 775.20 and included three key price relationships:

.382 retracement of the 723.10 low to the 806.50 high = 774.60 (point 1 to point 4)

.618 retracement of the 755.50 low to the 806.50 high = 775.00 (point 3 to point 4)

1.0 projection of the 786.80 high to the 755.50 low, projected from the 806.50 high = 775.20 (point 2 to point 3 projected from point 4)

The actual low was made at 775.50, which was within 3 ticks of the top of the cluster zone—an acceptable margin. A full 34-point rally followed this cluster setup.

The cluster illustrated in Figure 6-15 was developed on the daily cash SPX chart. This price cluster came in at the 1401.75–1405.07 area that included the coincidence of at least five price relationships:

.382 retracement of the 1360.98 low to the 1431.81 high = 1404.75 (point 2 to point 5)

.50 retracement of the 1377.83 low to the 1431.81 high = 1404.82 (point 4 to point 5)

1.272 extension of the 1410.28 low to the 1429.42 high = 1405.07 (point 6 to point 7)

1.0 projection of the 1407.89 high to the 1377.83 low, projected from the 1431.81 high = 1401.75 (point 3 to point 4 projected from point 5)

1.0 projection of the 1389.45 high to the 1360.98 low, projected from the 1431.81 high = 1403.34 (point 1 to point 2 projected from point 5)

The low was made directly within the cluster zone at the 1403.97 level. A rally of 36.72 followed.

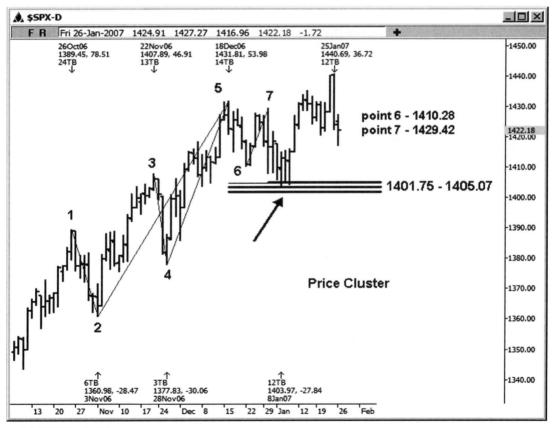

FIGURE 6-15

This next example is a five-minute chart of the March 2007 E-mini S&P contract (see Figure 6-16). Here we have a cluster of three Fibonacci price relationships at the 1443.75–1444.25 area:

.618 retracement of point 2 to point 4 = 1444.25

1.272 price extension of point 3 to point 4 = 1444.00

1.0 projection of point 1 to point 2 projected from point 4 = 1443.75

The market was in a general uptrend on this chart. The actual low in this case was made at 1444.00. The initial rally off this low ran for 7.75 points, or a value of $387.50.

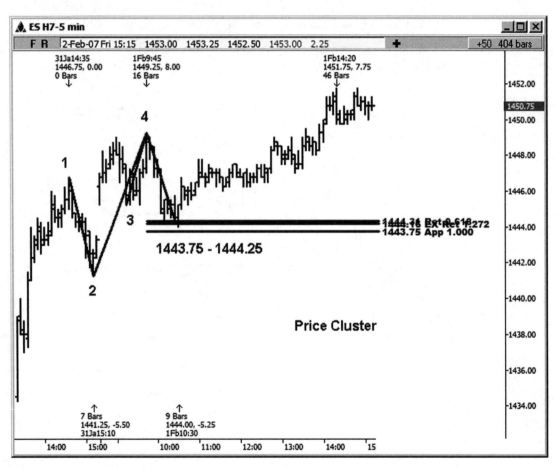

FIGURE 6-16

80

Let's take a look at an example in GM stock (see Figure 6-17). There was a confluence of three price relationships between 30.00 and 30.07:

.382 retracement of point 1 to point 5 = 30.07

.786 retracement of point 4 to point 5 = 30.00

1.0 projection of point 2 to point 3 projected from point 5 = 30.06

This was one of the higher-probability setups, since the cluster developed in the direction of the uptrend visible on the daily chart. The actual low was made at 30.10, just pennies above the high end of the cluster. It was followed by an initial rally of $3.90.

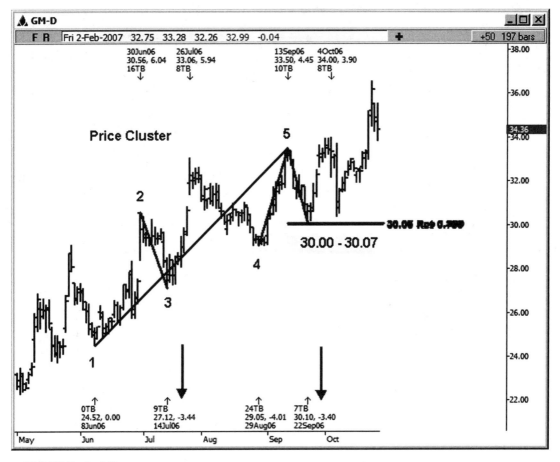

FIGURE 6-17

81

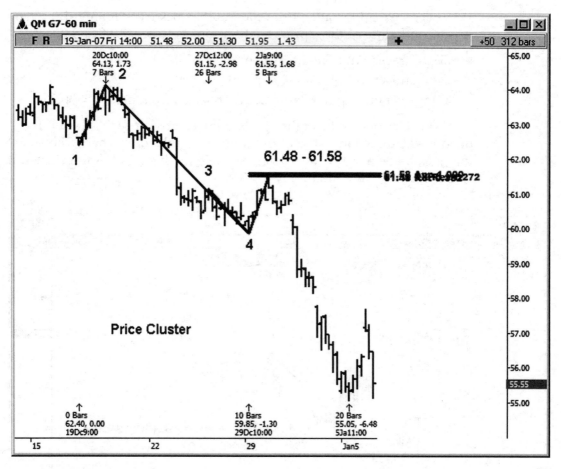

FIGURE 6-18

Figure 6-18 is an example of a 60-minute chart in the mini crude futures February 2007 contract. We were looking at a downtrending market here, so ideally we wanted to set up the resistance or "sell" clusters. A confluence of price relationships came in between 61.48 and 61.58.

.382 retracement of the 64.13 high to the 59.85 low (point 2 to point 4) = 61.48

1.272 extension of the 61.15 high to the 59.85 low (point 3 to point 4) = 61.50

100 percent projection of the 62.40 low to the 64.13 high, projected from the 59.85 low (point 1 to point 2 projected from point 4) = 61.58

The actual high in this case was made at 61.53. This cluster high was followed by a $6.48 decline in just a few trading sessions.

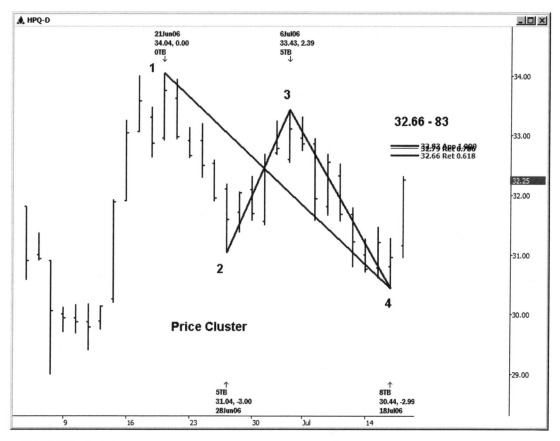

FIGURE 6-19

So far I'm pretty happy with my HP computers, so I decided to take a look at that company's daily stock chart for some market geometry. In Figure 6-19, we needed only four points to run the price relationships. A price cluster developed in the 32.66–32.83 area. In most of my chart examples, I've attempted to make the charts clean and avoid showing the overlapping price relationships, which typically make prices very difficult to read. However, that is exactly what we are looking for in a price cluster. We *love* it when the prices overlap nicely. It means that we have a beautiful confluence of price relationships. (It's hard to explain to your editor that the prices are supposed to be unreadable! I've chosen *not* to doctor up this example to show you what it should look like.)

The price relationships that defined this cluster were:

.618 retracement of the 6/21/06 high to the 7/18/06 low = 32.66 (point 1 to point 4)

.786 retracement of the 7/6/06 high to the 7/18/06 low = 32.79
 (point 3 to point 4)

1.0 projection of the 6/28/06 low to the 7/6/06 high, projected from
 the 7/18/06 low = 32.83 (point 2 to point 3 projected from point 4)

The market was rallying nicely into this key resistance decision.
Figure 6-20 will illustrate the results.

A high was made in HPQ at 32.76, which was directly within the price
cluster zone. This was followed pretty quickly by a decline of $2.78. If you
look closely at Figure 6-20, you can also see another good symmetry example
in addition to the one that was included in the price cluster zone. How about
the fact that the decline from the 6/21/06 high to the 6/28/06 low was a $3.00
decline, very similar to the decline from the 7/6/06 high to the 7/18/06 low,
which was $2.99? A rally of $2.32 followed this simple symmetry projection.

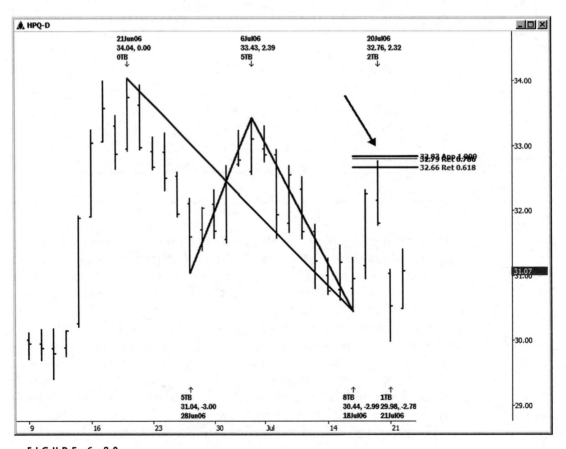

FIGURE 6-20

> **Author Tip** When someone tries to tell me that the markets are random, I always chuckle silently. It's not worth going through the argument with people who refuse to do their homework and actually study the geometry and patterns in the market. Beyond my mentor and other teachers, I have let the market teach me over the last 20 years or so. So far the market has not *lied* to me, and it has taught me quite a bit. I am still a humble student and continue to learn as time goes on.

There is one more lesson to be learned from the HPQ chart (see Figure 6-21). Although we did see a nice reaction off the original price cluster example at the 32.66–32.83 area, do *not* get stuck on a directional opinion. Use a trailing stop to protect your profits when you are in a good trade setup. Don't assume that the setup will continue working for you

FIGURE 6-21

indefinitely or that it *has* to at least make the initial 1.272 target (29.81 in this case). What the market giveth, the market can take away rather quickly. In other words, be flexible.

This last price cluster setup fell a bit short of the 1.272 target at 29.81, with the low terminating the decline at 29.98. A rather important trend change was seen after this low was made. As long as you used a trailing stop in this trade, you would have walked away with a nice profit. If, however, you had made the assumption that the price would make the 1.272 target, you might have given back much of the profits you had worked so hard for earlier.

The next example is of a price cluster that developed on a 15-minute chart in the March 2007 mini-sized Dow (see Figure 6-22). It included a coincidence of at least five Fibonacci price relationships between 12648 and 12655.

.236 retracement of point 3 to point 7 at 12654

.382 retracement of point 6 to point 7 at 12648

1.0 projection of point 1 to point 2, projected from point 7 at 12655

1.0 projection of point 4 to point 5, projected from point 7 at 12653

1.618 extension of the 12667 swing low to the 12698 swing high at 12648

This last projection is illustrated in Figure 6-23, since it is difficult to see where it came from. Even though it was from a relatively minor swing on the chart, it was a good confirming extension that overlapped the cluster nicely.

Notice in Figure 6-22 that there were three corrective declines that were similar or equal (43, 45, and 43 points). When symmetry projections overlap other price relationships, it strengthens the value of the price cluster.

The actual low in this case was made at 12655, which was followed by at least a 59-point rally. Each point in the mini-sized Dow is worth $5.00 per contract.

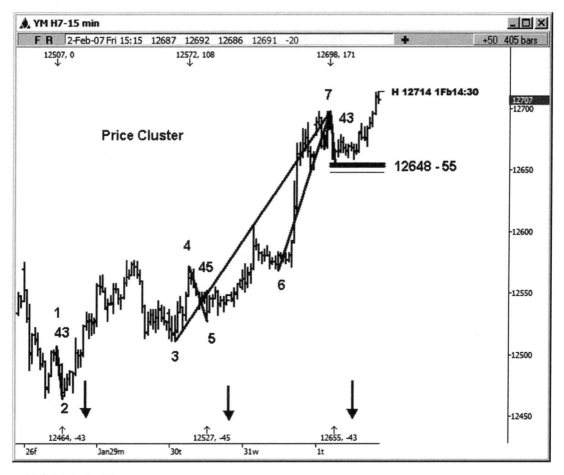

FIGURE 6-22

Figure 6-23 on the 15-minute mini-sized Dow shows where the minor extension at the 12648 area came from. (It was difficult to see on the previous chart, since it was overlapped by other price relationships.)

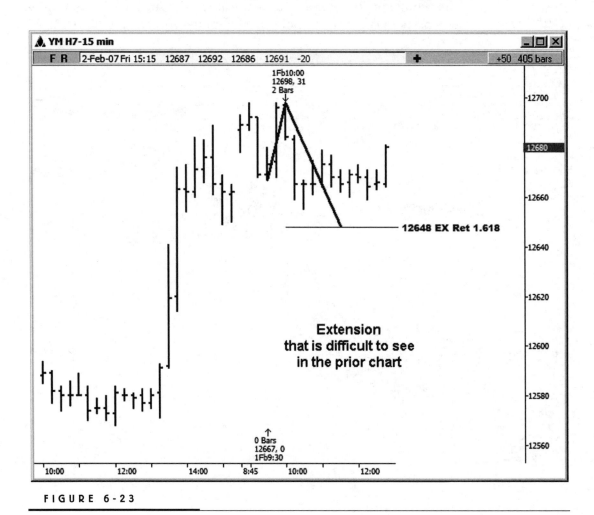

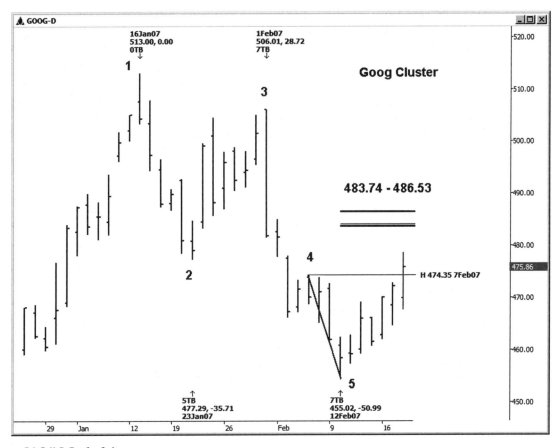

FIGURE 6-24

In Figure 6-24, the next price cluster example is done on a daily chart of Google. Here I was looking to set up some resistance, since we were looking at a bearish pattern, at that time with lower lows and lower highs. There was a coincidence of four price relationships in the 483.74–486.53 area.

.50 retracement of the 513.00 high to the 455.02 low = 484.01 (point 1 to point 5)

.618 retracement of the 506.01 high to the 455.02 low = 486.53 (point 3 to point 5)

1.618 extension of the 474.35 high to the 455.02 low = 486.30 (point 4 to point 5)

1.0 projection of the 477.29 low to the 506.01 high, projected from the 455.02 low = 483.74 (point 2 to point 3 projected from point 5)

Where I projected the 1.618 extension from might be a little difficult to see or understand. That swing actually might be more visible on a 60-minute chart. Eventually, you will be able to train your eye to find all possible swings that you can use to confirm a price zone as an important decision.

Figure 6-25 shows what happened around that key price cluster decision in Google. A high was made at 484.24, and it was followed by a $45.56 decline rather quickly. Once Google hit this resistance and failed to clear it, the trader would start looking for sell triggers to enter a short trade using this price cluster resistance.

FIGURE 6-25

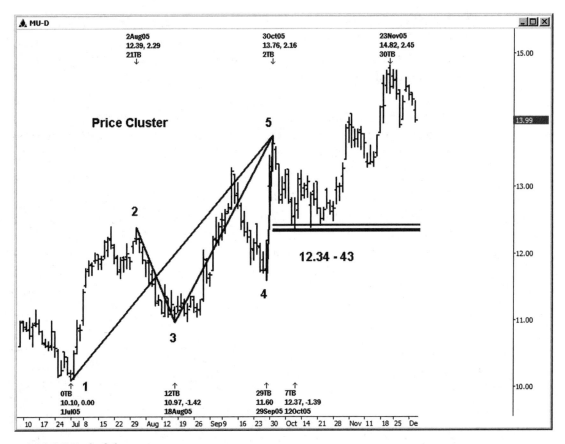

2Aug05
12.39, 2.29
21TB
↓

30ct05
13.76, 2.16
2TB
↓

23Nov05
14.82, 2.45
30TB

-15.00

Price Cluster

5

13.99

-13.00

2

12.34 - 43

-12.00

4

-11.00

3

1
0TB
10.10, 0.00
1Jul05

↑
12TB
10.97, -1.42
18Aug05

↑
29TB
11.60
29Sep05

↑
7TB
12.37, -1.39
12Oct05

-10.00

10 17 '24 Jul 8   15   22   29   Aug 12   19   26   Sep9   16   23   30   Oct 14   21   28   Nov 11   18 25   De

F I G U R E   6 - 2 6

Micron Technologies gives us a good price cluster example on a daily chart. The support cluster illustrated in Figure 6-26 was first tested on 10/12/05. The cluster developed between the 12.34–12.43 area from the following price relationships:

.382 retracement of the 7/1/05 low to the 10/3/05 high = 12.36 (point 1 to point 5)

.50 retracement of the 8/18/05 low to the 10/3/05 high = 12.37 (point 3 to point 5)

.618 retracement of the 9/29/05 low to the 10/3/05 high = 12.43 (point 4 to point 5)

1.0 projection of the 8/2/05 high to the 8/18/05 low, projected from the 10/3/05 high = 12.34 (point 2 to point 3 projected from point 5)

An important low was made at 12.37, which was directly within the price cluster zone. We saw an eventual move to 14.82 from this low.

Author Tip   Note that I haven't numbered the highs and lows in these next few examples. By now you should have an idea of what we're doing, and you can still see where the price relationships were projected from by following the dates on the chart.

Here is a nice little cluster on a daily chart of Honeywell stock that developed in the 41.38–41.56 area (see Figure 6-27). This cluster includes the coincidence of four price relationships:

.382 retracement of the 9/11/06 low to the 12/5/06 high = 41.56

.786 retracement of the 10/19/06 low to the 12/5/06 high = 41.42

1.272 extension of the 11/28/06 low to the 12/5/06 high = 41.38

1.0 projection of the 10/18/06 high to the 10/19/06 low, projected from the 12/5/06 high = 41.45

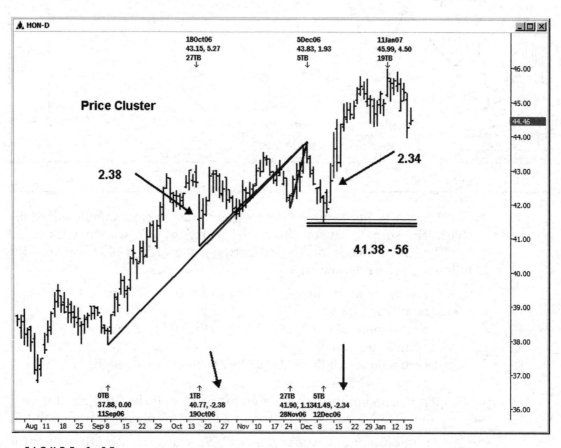

FIGURE 6-27

92

Another thing to notice on this chart is how the two labeled corrective swings were very similar. One swing was $2.38 and the second into the cluster zone was $2.34. The low in HON was made at 41.49, with a $4.50 rally eventually following that low.

The next price cluster example we are looking at is a daily chart of Merck (see Figure 6-28). With the general pattern of lower lows and lower highs, this is where it would be to your advantage to set up a price cluster on the sell side to agree with the trend of MRK at that time. A cluster with the minimum of three price relationships developed in the 29.44–29.76 area.

.618 retracement of the 7/18/05 high to the 8/22/05 low = 29.76

.50 retracement of the 8/10/05 high to the 8/22/05 low = 29.67

1.0 projection of the 7/7/05 low to the 7/18/05 high, projected from the 8/22/05 low = 29.44

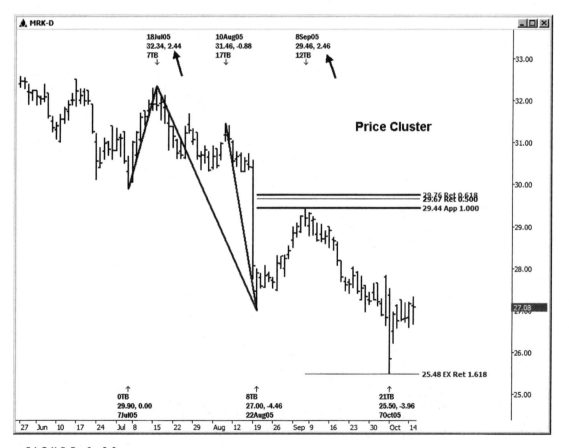

FIGURE 6-28

Notice the symmetry (similarity or equality) of the prior corrective rally to the 7/18/05 high (2.44) and the rally to the 9/8/05 high in the cluster zone (2.46). The high in this case was made just a couple of cents above the low end of the price cluster zone at 29.46 on 9/8/05. This trade setup essentially made the second price target when a $3.96 decline was seen from the price cluster high. Target 2 came in with the 1.618 extension at the 25.48 level. The 25.50 low was just 2 cents short of this level.

This next price cluster, in General Motors, comes from a coincidence of three key price relationships between 30.00 and 30.08 (see Figure 6-29). You may recognize this chart from the earlier chapter on retracements where I illustrated the .236 retracement by itself. Even though some traders might feel comfortable trading using a single price retracement, I think you would prefer to know that there were at least two more overlapping price relationships in that area!

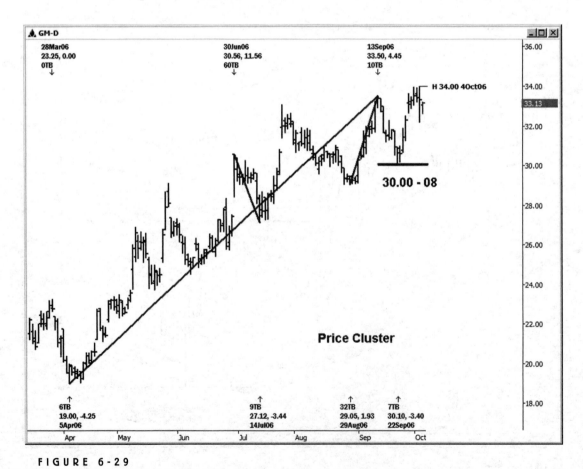

FIGURE 6-29

The price relationships in the zone were:

.236 retracement of the 4/5/06 low to the 9/13/06 high = 30.08

.786 retracement of the 8/29/06 low to the 9/13/06 high = 30.00

1.0 projection of the 6/30/06 high to the 7/14/06 low, projected from the 9/13/06 high = 30.06

A low was made at 30.10, just 2 cents above the high end of the cluster zone. This low was followed by a rally of $3.90.

Figure 6-30 is a reminder that price clusters don't always hold! This is a daily cash chart of the Russell index. There were two key support clusters that stood out on the chart: a zone between 755.40 and 757.57, and then one between 753.06 and 753.32. The clusters developed from symmetry

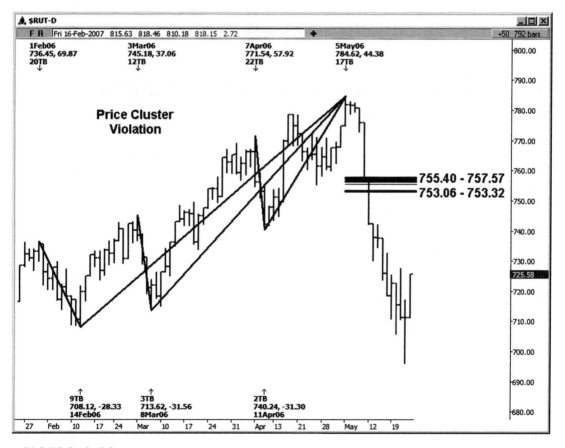

FIGURE 6-30

projections of prior corrective declines along with multiple retracements of the prior swings labeled on the chart. Neither one of these cluster zones held.

As a matter of fact, there are many price clusters that are violated each and every day in this market. You should not expect every cluster zone to hold. We simply want to look at possible trade entries using the ones that do hold, and where we see an actual entry trigger. (Entry triggers will be discussed in a later chapter.)

This chapter walked you through the process of setting up Fibonacci price clusters. These trade setups are very well defined as far as your risk is concerned, along with the definition of a minimum trade target that you can look for if a trade entry is triggered. Even though many of these price cluster zones are violated every day, the ones that hold and trigger offer you a relatively low-risk, high-probability trade setup with excellent risk/reward parameters.

7 CHAPTER

SYMMETRY—THE POWER TOOL: TRADE SETUP 2

Let's take a deeper look at the concept of *symmetry* and how we use it as a trade setup. Once again, my definition of symmetry is similarity or "equality" when comparing swings in the same direction. This is a simple, yet very powerful trading tool that should not be overlooked. I'm not going to tell you that I discovered this technique. Many market masters already use these projections. Most commonly it is also called a measured move.

To identify symmetry, I have been using the price projection tool with the 1.0 setting. (This is sometimes called an extension tool on many other analysis programs.) With projections, we are comparing swings in the same direction by using this tool, which allows you to choose three price points to make the projection. I use symmetry *most* often to project possible support or resistance in order to help me enter a trade in the direction of the trend. This is where trade setup 2 comes in. To create these setups, I project 100 percent of the prior corrective swings to help identify areas to enter the market in the direction of the trend. What I mean by *corrective swings* is the countertrend or shorter-term declines within a larger uptrend, or the countertrend or shorter-term rallies within a larger downtrend.

As far as my trading plan goes, *only symmetry that is projected from a prior corrective swing within a larger trend qualifies as a trade setup.* I define the trend by the pattern on the chart. If I'm looking at a pattern of higher highs and higher lows, I'm looking at setting up the symmetry trades on the buy side. If I'm looking at a pattern of lower lows and lower highs, I'm looking at setting up the symmetry trades on the sell side. One level is sufficient for a setup, although sometimes you will see multiple symmetry projections that overlap the same general area.

Symmetry can also be projected from swings in the direction of the larger trend to help determine areas where a trend move might terminate. I use these symmetry projections only to help in exiting trades, or as an area where I start to recommend tightening up stops on a position. Personally, I do *not* consider using these symmetry projections for a trade setup, since the projections of the main trend are actually setting up a trade that is countertrend.

Author Tip Some traders may still use these projections for a trade; however, countertrend trading is not for beginners or for those who are not nimble. Personally, I prefer to focus on the setups that have you enter the market in the direction of the main trend after a corrective move. This helps to keep the odds in your favor.

The trade targets and stops will essentially be the same for a symmetry setup as they are for a price cluster setup. We will be looking for 1.272 of the prior swing into the symmetry projection(s) or levels as a minimum target, and the maximum risk would be a few ticks above or below the symmetry projection(s).

SYMMETRY EXAMPLES

The first symmetry example, Figure 7-1, is illustrated on a three-minute chart of the March 2007 E-mini Russell contract. I have labeled the swings that are similar on this chart. Within one larger swing up in this contract from 783.10 to 790.20, we can see swings down of 1.50, 1.90, 1.60, and 1.70 points. These swings fit the definition of symmetry, as they are all similar. Since they are within the context of an uptrend, I am also considering these to be corrective swings. A trade setup could have been created in a couple of places on this chart, as the prior corrective declines would have been projected from any new high to identify a possible buy entry.

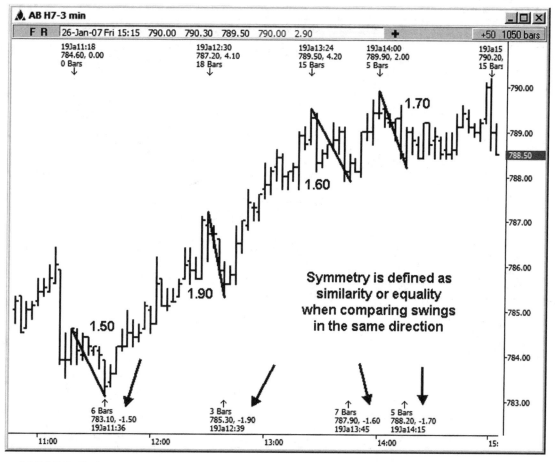

FIGURE 7-1

Figure 7-2 is a symmetry example on a daily FOREX chart of USD/CAD (U.S. dollar/Canadian dollar). I have labeled the similar swings on this chart. The swing of 211 pips is similar to the 206-point pips. The swing of 160 pips is similar to the 158-pip swing. In this case, there are two separate examples of symmetry within this chart. The swings that are compared in this chart are also considered corrective moves within the daily uptrend. An example of symmetry setup on this chart would be to use the move from the 12/18/06 high to the 12/20/06 low (160 pips) and project it from the 1/11/07 high using the 1.0 setting on the projection tool. This would have set up 1.1644 as possible support and a buy entry zone.

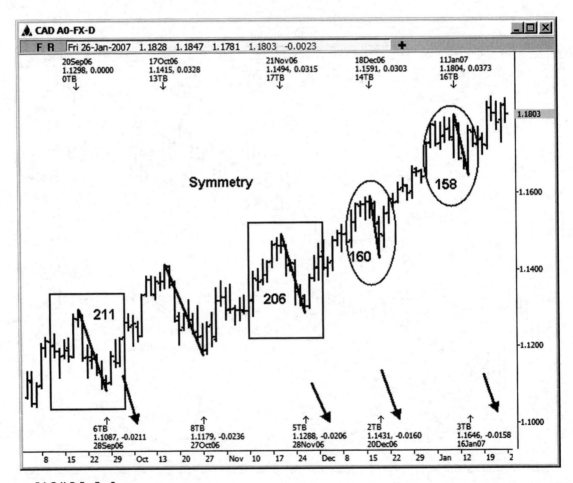

FIGURE 7-2

The actual low was made at 1.1646 and was followed by a relatively healthy rally.

In Figure 7-3, we are looking at the 60-minute March 2007 bond contract. Notice that the first swing identified on the chart was 26/32nds. Once this was projected from the 110 08/32nd swing low, it showed us possible "symmetry resistance" at the 111 02/32nd area. That was the trade setup. In this case, the rally from the 110 08/32nd low terminated *exactly* at the symmetry projection. Remember, symmetry is similarity or *equality*. The bond dropped almost 2 full points from that high.

FIGURE 7-3

A major low was made on the daily Nasdaq cash on 7/18/06. After this low was made, we can find quite a few examples of symmetry in Figure 7-4. The corrections that I've labeled here are 48.08, 53.56, 42.15, 46.85, 42.96, and 52.60. Notice the similarity between some of these swings within the uptrend. There were at least a couple of potential symmetry trade setups on this chart.

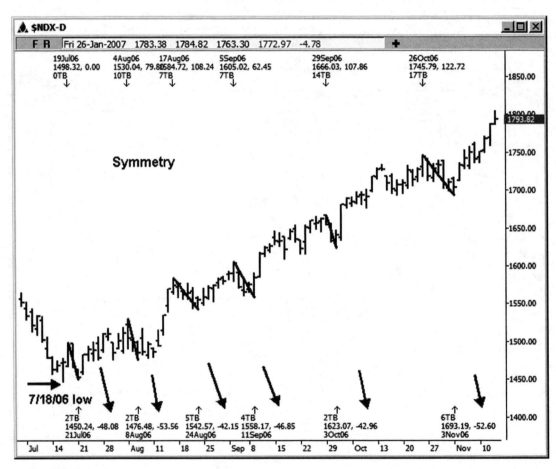

FIGURE 7-4

Let's look at one of these symmetry examples within that same Nasdaq chart. It would have proved to be a healthy trade setup in the direction of the trend (see Figure 7-5). Although there may have been other price relationships that overlapped this symmetry projection, we are just going to focus on the symmetry itself in this example. If you measure the corrective swing from the 8/4/06 high to the 8/8/06 low and project 100 percent of this swing from the 10/26/06 high, 1692.23 becomes the possible support decision and the setup. The actual low was made just a touch above this key projection. A gorgeous rally followed, with an initial runup from 1693.19 to 1824.21, or 131.02 points.

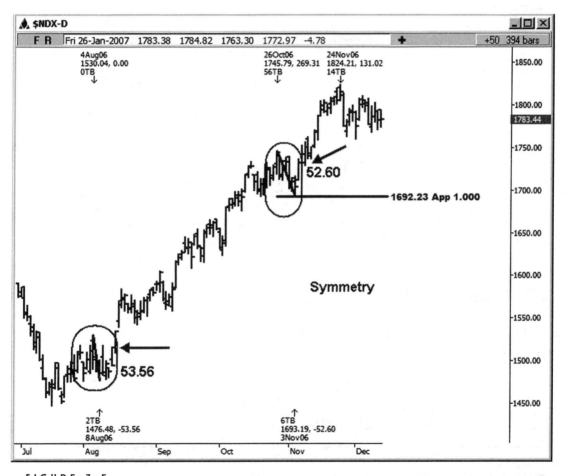

FIGURE 7-5

It is definitely worth it to keep an eye on the symmetry projections from higher time frame charts. Figure 7-6 is a weekly FOREX chart in the euro (euro/U.S. dollar). Symmetry helped to identify a major swing low in this market. The first decline labeled on the chart was an 1167 pip swing down. This 1167 pip decline was then projected down from the high made the week of 2/20/04. The result was a projection of possible support around the 1.1761 area. That was the trade setup. The actual low was made at 1.1760 within one pip of the symmetry projection. A huge rally of 1907 pips eventually followed this low.

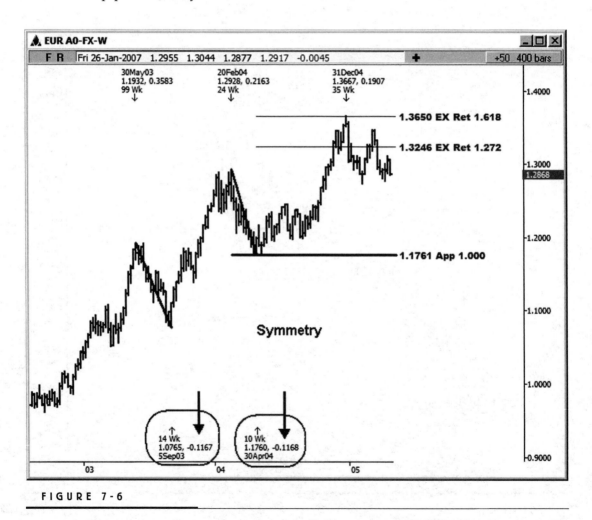

FIGURE 7-6

Figure 7-7 is a daily chart of the cash Dow Jones Industrial Average. Between the week of 3/11/05 and the week of 4/22/05, the Dow traveled down 984.00 points from the high to the low. From the week of 5/12/06 to the week of 7/21/06, the Dow traveled down 986.87 points from the high to the low. A symmetry projection from that May 2006 high helped to identify support in the Dow, from which an extremely healthy rally eventually unfolded. This projection qualified as another great symmetry setup.

FIGURE 7-7

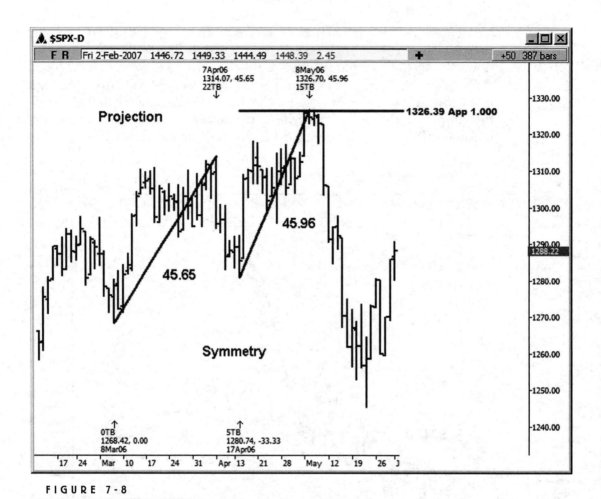

FIGURE 7-8

This next symmetry example is on a daily S&P cash chart. Figure 7-8 illustrates a symmetry projection that was made from swings in the direction of the main trend, which at that time was up. This projection identified possible resistance to the rally. Since the main trend was up into this resistance zone, looking to enter the short side of this market using this zone would be considered a countertrend trade when the resistance zone was first tested. If you measured from the 3/8/06 low to the 4/7/06 high (45.65 points) and you projected 100 percent from the 4/17/06 low, you came up with possible symmetry resistance at the 1326.39 area. The actual high was made at 1326.70.

These swings were very similar, and they indicated an area where the rally might terminate. In such a case, you would want to tighten stops on any long positions. Even though the odds for entering a trade using a countertrend projection are lower than those when you use these projections within the direction of the trend, the projections can still be extremely valuable. It is just very important to wait for clear reversal indications on a lower time frame chart so that you are not stepping in front of the proverbial freight train.

If I am looking at a daily chart zone, I like to see a shift in pattern on a 15-minute chart or higher to indicate a trend reversal. So, according to my trading plan, I am not allowed to sell short on a first test of the zone in this example. If the 15-minute chart shows me a pattern reversal however (in this case to lower lows and lower highs), then I can set up a sell entry that will be legal on my trading plan.

Figure 7-9 is a symmetry example illustrated on the March 2007 E-mini Russell contract. Here I measured from the 11/28/06 low to the 12/5/06 high, which was a 34.10-point swing. This same distance was then projected from the 1/9/07 low, looking for possible resistance. The symmetry projection came in at 807.30. The actual high was made at 807.10, making the second swing 33.90 points. This resistance did produce a tradable high. I don't consider this a trade setup according to my plan. It would have been a great place to tighten up stops or exit if you were long going into that resistance.

Again, my trading plan doesn't allow me to step in front of the freight train using that projection. Once the pattern on a 15-minute chart shifted to lower lows and lower highs, however, then I could finally look to safely set up the sell side with the 1/16/07 high in mind.

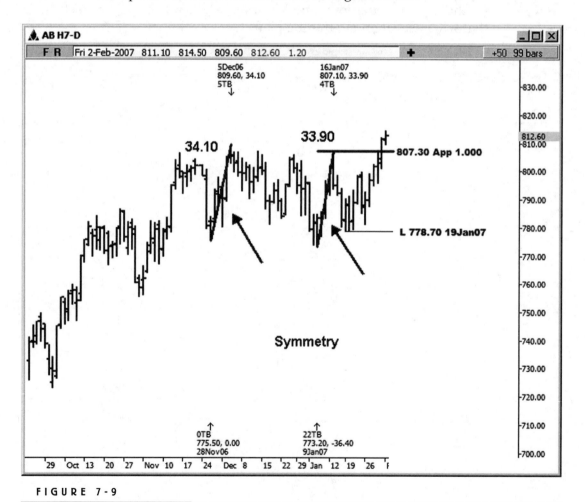

FIGURE 7-9

Author Tip Just keep in mind that using projections that are counter to the trend for trade entries has lower odds than using projections that show up in the direction of the trend.

Figure 7-10 is a daily chart of the Swissy (U.S. dollar/Swiss franc). Notice the similarity of the swings on this chart. The labels show rallies of 334 pips, 324 pips, and 323 pips. This fits the classic definition of symmetry.

FIGURE 7-10

When I took a peek at the wheat market, I found some beautiful symmetry examples. These examples are illustrated on the daily March 2007 wheat contract. Who says there is no rhyme or reason to the market? Take a look at this first wheat chart (see Figure 7-11). Look at the similarity of the rallies in this contract. The labeled swings were $43^1/_2$ cents, $39^1/_2$ cents, 43 cents, 43 cents again, and 39 cents.

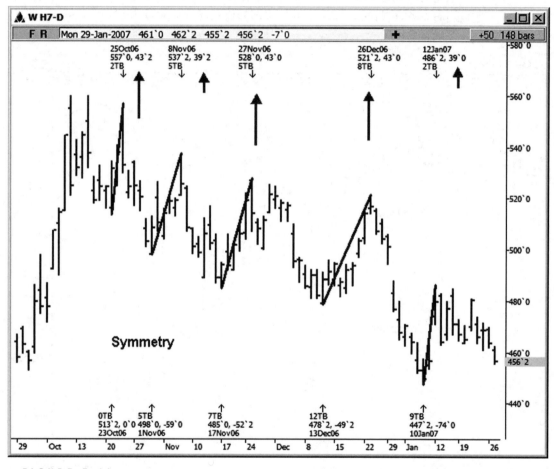

FIGURE 7-11

Let's look at another wheat chart (see Figure 7-12). Two of the prior swings in the earlier chart helped to create a beautiful price cluster setup that included symmetry at the 518–522 area. The decline that followed amounted to 74 cents in just a few weeks. That would be a huge score for a grain trader! Two of the price relationships in this cluster were simply 100 percent projections of prior rallies, one that lasted $43^1/2$ cents and another that was 43 cents. They just happened to overlap a couple of other Fibonacci price relationships, creating a healthy price cluster. The symmetry projections by themselves would have been considered a trade setup. The addition of the other price relationships strengthened the setup.

FIGURE 7-12

Figure 7-13 illustrates another simple symmetry setup that occurred on a 45-minute chart in the March 2007 miNY crude oil contract. In this example, there was perfect symmetry between the first and second swings identified on the chart. These swings both lasted $2.58. The projection told us to look for possible support at the 52.08 area; that was the setup. The low made at 52.08 was followed by a rally that was just over $3.00 per contract.

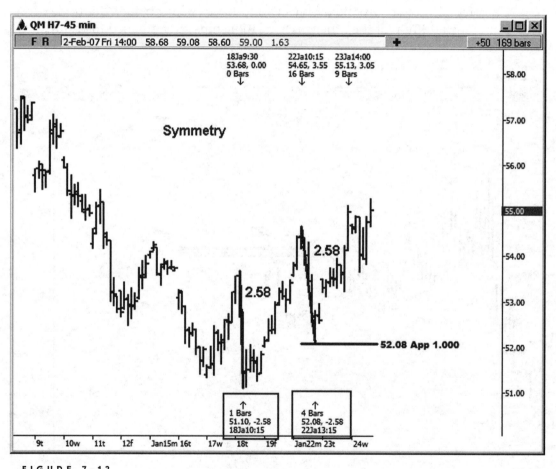

FIGURE 7-13

VIOLATIONS OR BREAKS IN SYMMETRY

Symmetry identifies some great trade setups. When it holds, it provides information to trade off of. When symmetry breaks or is violated, it also provides you with information that can help you in your trading. What I mean by broken or violated is when a market doesn't hold within a few ticks above or below the symmetry projections of prior corrective swings. The following chart examples will illustrate the importance of these violations and what they suggest will occur next in the market.

FIGURE 7-14

When symmetry is broken or violated, as in the daily chart of GM shown in Figure 7-14, a high percentage of the time you will see at least a deeper downside correction and sometimes a more important change in trend.

> **Author Tip**   Important trend changes will most often be preceded by a break in symmetry. This is something that you will want to keep in the back of your mind. There are actually traders in my room who will take a violation of symmetry on a lower time frame as a trade trigger to a higher time frame setup.

Notice in Figure 7-14 that once all the symmetry projections between 35.21 and 35.91 in GM on this daily chart were violated, a relatively dramatic reversal to the downside followed. You won't always see a dramatic reversal, but you certainly want to be aware of the possibility of this occurring when symmetry breaks.

The symmetry projections I used were made from all the obvious corrective declines since the prior major rally swing started in late November. I have identified these corrective declines in Figure 7-14. So when I'm talking about a symmetry break or violation in this case, I am saying that the market has declined more than *all* of the prior corrective declines, which were 1.59, 1.34, 2.03, and 1.33. In this case that means once we declined more than 2.03 from the 2/13/07 high by a decent margin, the symmetry of the last bull swing was violated.

In the daily U.S. dollar/Swiss franc (Swissy) FOREX chart in Figure 7-15, you can see that when the symmetry resistance projections from the prior major high-to-low swing were violated, this market started to make a deeper upside correction.

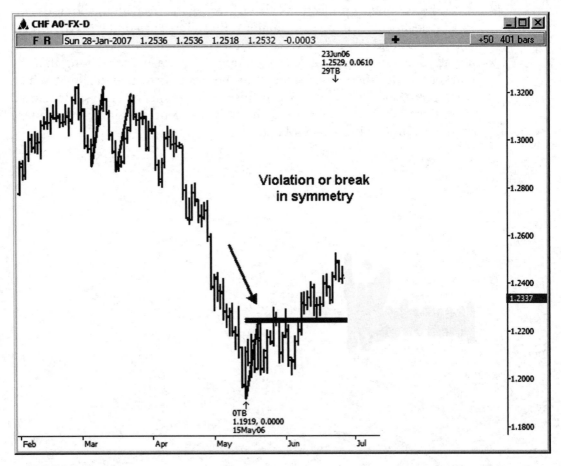

FIGURE 7-15

Figure 7-16 illustrates that the symmetry break in the previous chart was actually the beginning of a more important trend change. After the break in symmetry, you can see a shift in pattern to higher highs and higher lows. A rather healthy rally followed this break in symmetry.

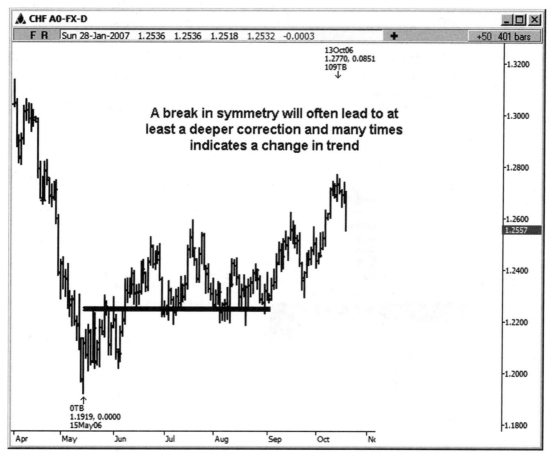

FIGURE 7-16

Let's take a look at an example of a symmetry break on a 15-minute chart of the March 2007 mini-sized Dow contract (see Figure 7-17). Note the corrective declines labeled on the left-hand side of the chart. They were 31, 25, 44, 28, and 32 points. When the new high was made on this chart, those swings were projected from that high where we would typically be looking for possible support on the pullback. Some of the projections clustered together in a relatively tight zone. One of the projections was a bit below that cluster. When all of the symmetry projections were violated on this chart of the prior major low-to-high swing, we knew that it indicated at least a deeper downside correction, and possibly a more important change in trend. (Knowing that might help a trader manage his or her positions more effectively.) A rather dramatic reversal followed this violation of the bullish symmetry projections.

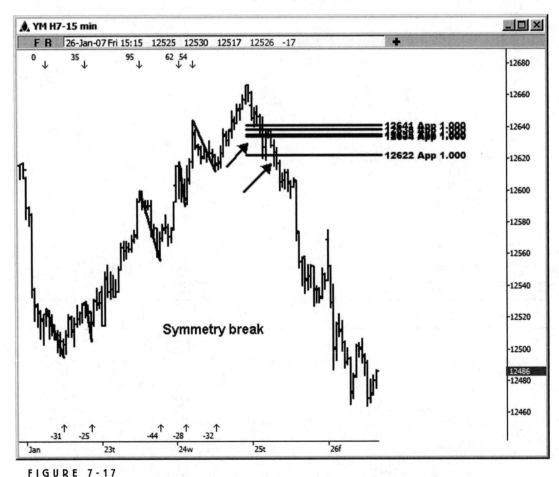

FIGURE 7-17

This next symmetry example is illustrated on a 15-minute E-mini S&P chart (see Figure 7-18). In this case, we saw only a bit of a deeper correction before the original trend resumed. The first decline was 4.00 points. The second decline, after the break in symmetry, was 6.50 points. So keep in mind that these breaks do not *always* indicate a more important change in trend.

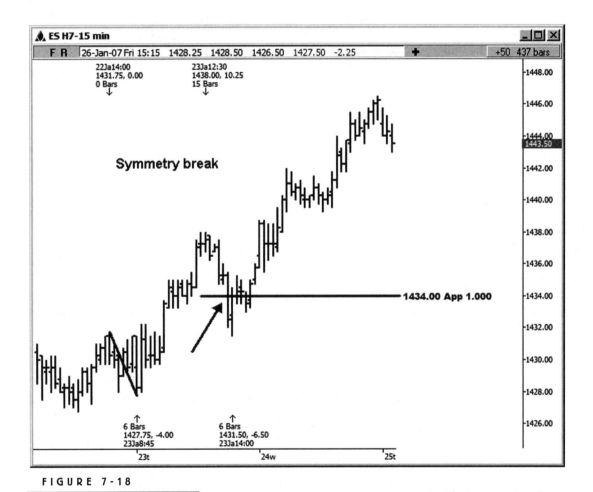

FIGURE 7-18

FIGURE 7-19

In the daily chart of Harley Davidson in Figure 7-19, you should be able to see, by just eyeballing the chart, that symmetry was violated after the 11/22/06 high was made. We were running these symmetry projections of the corrective declines of the prior major swing up from the 6/7/06 low to the 11/22/06 high. In this case, I also included a swing down just prior to the 6/7/06 low. I find that sometimes including a swing just before the new major trend begins can be a valuable projection. To define this violation of symmetry mathematically, once this stock corrected more than 3.57 down from any high, all the symmetry projections made on this chart were violated. Note that the largest corrective decline was 3.57. The other swings were similar, with 3.36, 3.55, and 3.32 declines. I consider symmetry to be violated once the largest symmetry projection was violated by a decent margin.

Even though this stock retraced nicely back toward that high, a rather healthy decline eventually ensued after this symmetry break. After symmetry is violated and the market pulls back, you want to watch for a possible failure and entry in the direction of the symmetry break.

Author Tip Although most of the symmetry projections made in this analysis are of prior corrective declines, as in the HOG chart example, there are times when I will include a projection from a swing just prior to development of the new trend. On that particular chart, the swing in question was from the 5/26/06 high to the 6/7/06 low. The projection was still a comparison of a similar swing in the same direction, though it was not considered a corrective swing of the move from the 6/7/06 low to the 11/22/06 high because it occurred prior to the new trend that started from the 6/7/06 low.

On this daily Nasdaq futures chart (see Figure 7-20), notice that I have labeled two prior declines. One of the declines was 50.50 points, and the other was 46.75 points. I projected both of these declines from the high made on 2/22/07, which showed me the possible symmetry support from which a rally could have resumed. Instead of holding above the key support of these projections at 1807.00–1810.75, symmetry support was violated, and this was followed by a relatively dramatic decline. Again, this won't happen every time symmetry is violated, but it is important to be aware of the possibilities at all times.

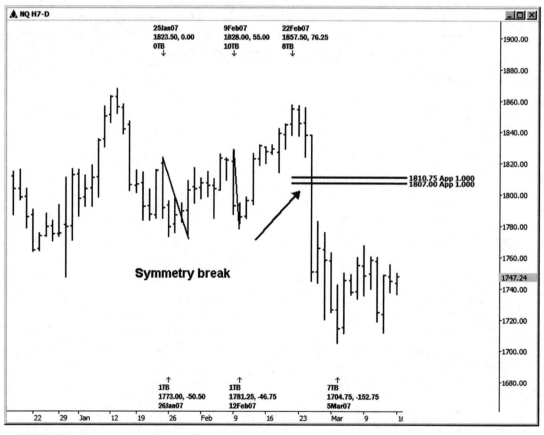

FIGURE 7-20

This next example illustrated on a daily chart of the electronic bond contract, shows another symmetry violation (see Figure 7-21). The initial violation was not by a huge margin, but it was visible enough to then watch for a possible change in the downtrend from the 12/1/06 high. After symmetry is violated, I will often start watching the next pullback for a possible market entry, since a change of trend is often seen after a symmetry break.

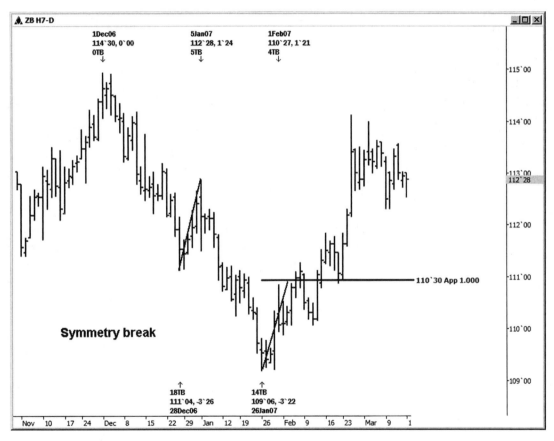

FIGURE 7-21

The next bond chart (see Figure 7-22) shows you where you could have watched the pullback after the symmetry break for a possible buy entry. In this example, the bond pulled back to just a couple of ticks above the .618 retracement. This was the beginning of a healthy trend reversal in the bond when the rally resumed from above this retracement.

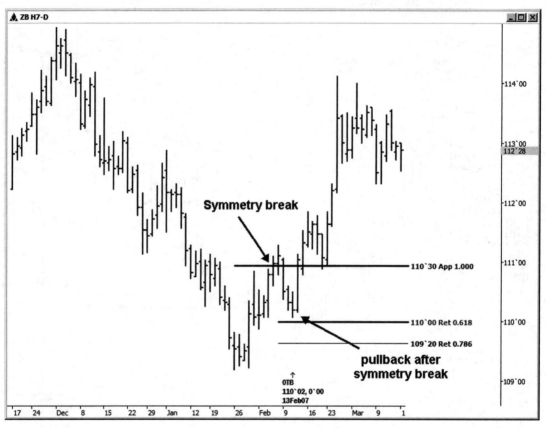

FIGURE 7-22

This chapter on symmetry showed you how to use these symmetry or 1.0 price projections as a simple yet powerful trade setup. It also discussed what we should look for when the symmetry of a market swing is violated. Along with price cluster setups, symmetry trade setups also offer relatively low-risk trades with a healthy risk/reward ratio.

8
C H A P T E R

THE TWO-STEP PATTERN SETUP: TRADE SETUP 3

Patterns tend to repeat themselves, both in life and in the marketplace. There is one particular pattern that I like to look for in all markets—a two-step pattern. I was first introduced to this pattern when I was studying the basics of Elliot wave analysis, where this pattern is considered a corrective or countertrend move that is seen before a trend resumes.

A two-step pattern can also be called a Gartley pattern, depending on the ratios that show up within it. The definition of a Gartley pattern is a bit more specific in terms of the ratios that show up within the pattern. For this reason, not all two-step patterns will fit the definition of a Gartley pattern, although all Gartley patterns are considered to be two-step patterns. (For more information on the Gartley pattern, check out *Fibonacci Ratios with Pattern Recognition* by Larry Pesavento.)

The two-step trade setup is a zigzag pattern that corrects a prior trend move. If we identify this pattern correctly, it should eventually resolve itself in the direction of the trend prior to the evolution of the zigzag. Within this pattern we will be looking for specific Fibonacci price relationships to overlap or *cluster* to make sure it falls within the definition of a proper two-step. These price relationships will be defined in this chapter.

(A two-step pattern can be a bullish setup, as in Figure 8-1, or a bearish setup, as in Figure 8-2.) So trade setup 3 is essentially a price cluster, with the addition of the zigzag pattern that strengthens the setup.

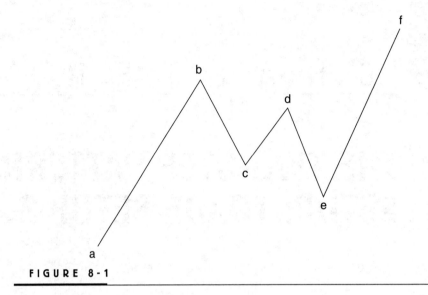

FIGURE 8-1

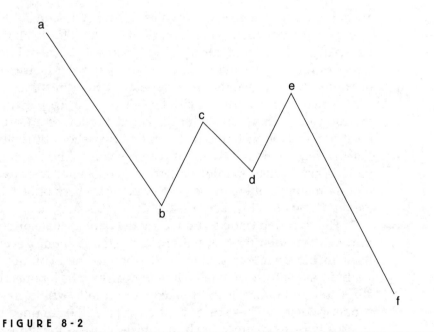

FIGURE 8-2

The actual zigzag pattern we are looking to identify occurs between points b and e. The ratios that we are going to run to look for a cluster will come from:

Running the retracements of a to b (.382, .50, .618, and .786)

Running the price extensions of c to d (1.272 and 1.618)

Running the price projection of b to c, projected from d (1.00)

The same ratios are applied to both bullish and bearish two-step patterns (see Figures 8-1 and 8-2).

Running these numbers will typically produce a price cluster of three Fibonacci price relationships that overlap each other nicely. Any of these price relationships can overlap; however, the two-step patterns that set up the ideal situation typically have a retracement ratio of either .618 or .786 from a to b that overlaps either a 1.272 or a 1.618 extension of the move from c to d that *also* overlaps a 100 percent projection of the first swing of the zigzag, which would mean that bc = de. I believe this ideal two-step fits the more stringent definition of a Gartley pattern. You might also see a two-step pattern develop in the market in which de = 1.618 of the b-to-c swing. I've found this to be a lot less common, so I have chosen not to include it in the definition of what I look for in my two-step pattern setups.

After these initial price relationships have been run, there may be additional Fibonacci price relationships that show up from other swings on the chart. This will just add strength to the setup and identify it as an important price decision.

WHY IS THIS A GOOD PATTERN?

My best explanation of why this pattern can be so lucrative comes from general swing theory. When we study basic technical analysis, we are generally taught that violating or taking out a prior swing low indicates weakness and/or a change in trend back to the downside. It would also follow that violating or taking out a prior swing high indicates strength and/or a change in trend back to the upside. Let's keep these basic technical concepts in mind as we examine the two-step pattern.

Within the zigzag pattern, when you take out point c, you are taking out either a prior swing high or a prior swing low. As discussed earlier, *this often signals a trend change.* For example, if point c was a low and the market traded below it, traders who follow swing theory might sell to exit long positions as a result of this violation. They might also sell to enter new short positions. In many cases, the market will just continue down, as the break of the prior swing low does often signal a trend change as swing theory suggests.

If you run the two-step price relationships, however, and the price ends up holding *above* them, you have to consider the possibility that the pattern may be a two-step and that the original trend will resume instead of a trend reversal unfolding.

So when you start to see a zigzag pattern, you have to ask yourself the question, is this a trend reversal or a two-step pattern? Initially you won't know the answer. The bottom line is, you will know the *levels* that will *need to hold* if the two-step pattern is going to play out, but not whether or not they will hold. The biggest clues as to whether or not a two-step pattern will play out are going to come from your trade filters and triggers which will be discussed later.

Now remember in this example all the traders who either exited their long positions or went short when the prior swing low was violated. If the two-step price support parameters end up holding and the bulls regain control, those who exited might buy to reestablish long positions, and those who sold short should be buying to get out of an unsatisfying short trade. This will hopefully drive up the prices and *pay* you on the two-step pattern setup that you correctly identified.

The maximum stop on a two-step pattern setup is the same as that on a price cluster setup (a few ticks above or below the extreme of the price cluster). The initial price target for the two-step pattern is a bit different, however. The initial trade target is always the 1.272 extension of the whole zigzag, which is represented by the swing of b to e.

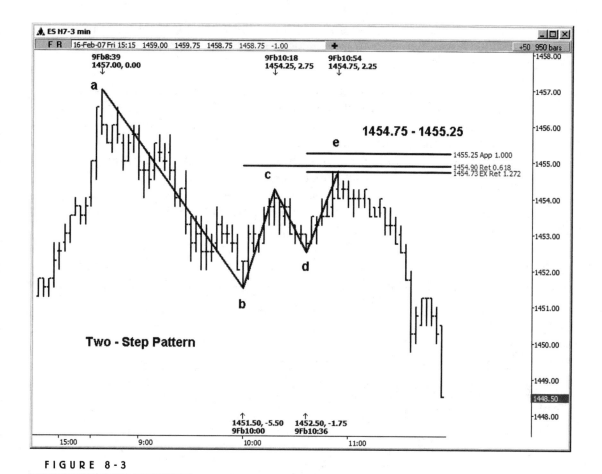

FIGURE 8-3

If you are a little *fuzzy* on the concept of the two-step pattern setup, the following examples should set you straight on what to look for. Let's start with an example of a bearish two-step pattern. Figure 8-3 is an example that was actually set up in my chat room on 2/9/07 on a three-minute E-mini S&P chart. The price relationships that made up this two-step pattern cluster included the .618 retracement of point a to point b, the 1.272 extension of point c to point d, and the 1.0 projection of b to point c, projected from point d:

.618 retracement of 1457.00 high to the 1451.50 low
(point a to point b) = 1454.90

1.272 extension of the 1454.25 high to the 1452.50 low
(point c to point d) = 1454.73

1.0 price projection of the 1451.50 low to the 1454.25 high, projected from the 1452.50 low (point b to point c, projected from point d) = 1455.25

I rounded the numbers from these projections to the closest futures price and labeled this cluster 1454.75–1455.25. The actual high was made at 1454.75, which was at the low end of the cluster. The initial downside target, which was the 1.272 extension of the move from point b to point e, came in at 1450.75. This first target was met along with the second and third targets of 1.618 and 2.618.

Figure 8-4 shows that an eventual decline of 17.75 points was seen from this first example of a two-step pattern high. It also illustrates what I mean by the zigzag pattern.

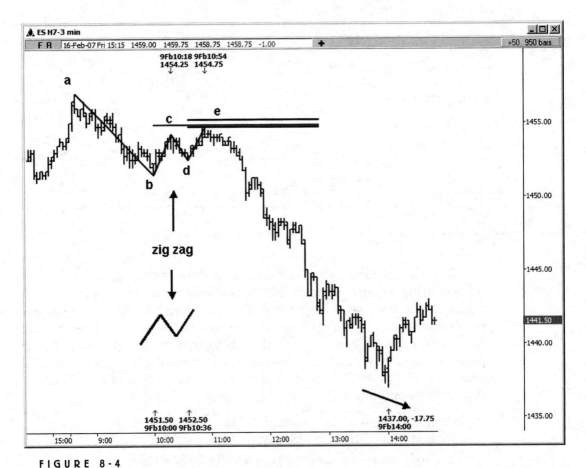

FIGURE 8-4

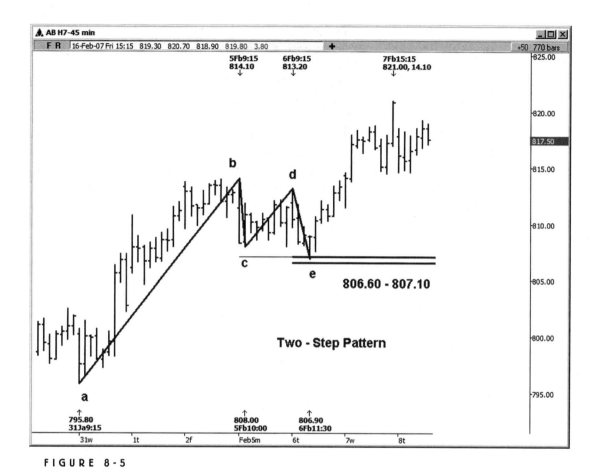

FIGURE 8-5

Figure 8-5 is an example of a bullish two-step pattern setup on a 45-minute chart in the E-mini Russell contract. The price cluster included the .382 retracement of point a to point b, the 1.272 extension of point c to point d, and the 1.0 projection of point b to point c, projected from point d:

.382 retracement of the 795.80 low to the 814.10 high
   (point a to point b) = 807.11

1.272 extension of the 808.00 low to the 813.20 high
   (point c to point d) = 806.59

1.0 projection of the 814.10 high to the 808.00 low, projected from the
   813.20 high (point b to point c, projected from point d) = 807.10

Again I rounded the numbers from the program to the closest futures price available and came up with a cluster zone at the 806.60–807.10 area. The actual low was made at 806.90. The initial rally from the two-step pattern low lasted 14.10 points. Also note that this two-step example is not as symmetrical as some of the other examples you may see develop in the markets. The swings from point b to point c and from point d to point e are rather short in time compared to the swing from point c to point d. Generally these swings are a bit more similar in time.

(As long as you can see the zigzag and the price relationships overlap to create the cluster, however, it is good enough for a trade setup in my book!)

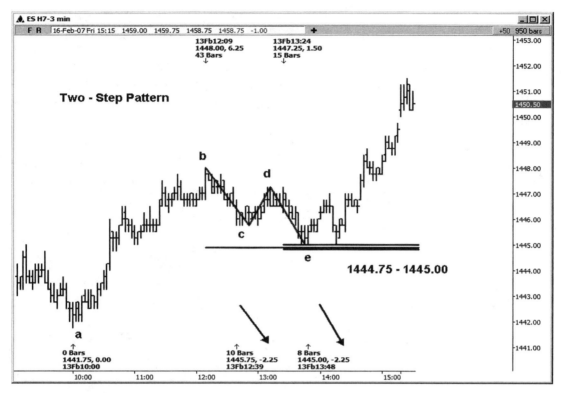

FIGURE 8-6

Let's look at another two-step pattern that developed in the E-mini S&P March 2007 contract on a three-minute chart (see Figure 8-6). The zigzag is labeled on the chart. The two-step pattern cluster developed from a 50 percent retracement of point a to point b, a 1.618 extension of point c to point d, and the 1.0 projection of point b to point c, projected from point d. This created a cluster in the 1444.75–1445.00 area.

.50 retracement of the 1441.75 low to the 1448.00 high
  (point a to point b) = 1444.88

1.618 extension of the 1445.75 low to the 1447.25 high
  (point c to point d) = 1444.82

1.0 projection of the 1448.00 high to the 1445.75 low, projected from
  1447.25 high (point b to point c, projected from point d) = 1445.00

Notice the equality of the swings from b to c and from d to e. Both of these swings were exactly 2.25 points. Symmetry is a big part of the ideal two-step pattern.

The actual low was made at 1445.00, as shown in Figure 8-7. This trade setup attained all three targets on the upside and continued even higher. A rally of 13.50 was seen from this low pretty quickly. There are many times when the market will surpass all trade targets. For this reason, I recommend using a trailing stop on at least part of your trading position so that you can fully take advantage of some of these extended moves that start with a very low risk trade setup.

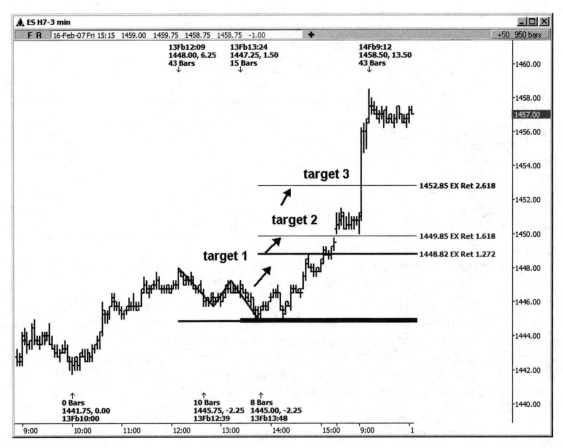

FIGURE 8-7

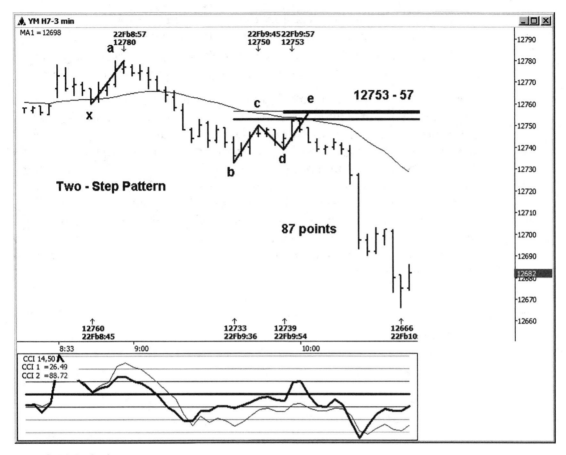

In Figure 8-8, we are looking at a two-step pattern on a three-minute chart of the mini-sized Dow contract. The price cluster came in at the 12753–12757 area.

The price relationships were:

.50 retracement of the 12780 high to the 12733 low
(point a to point b) = 12757

1.272 extension of the 12750 high to the 12739 low
(point c to point d) = 12753

1.618 extension of the 12750 high to the 12739 low
(point c to point d) = 12757

1.0 projection of the 12733 low to the 12750 high, projected from the 12739 low (point b to point c, projected from point d) = 12756

1.0 projection of the 12760 low to the 12780 high, projected from the 12733 low (point x to point a, projected from point b) = 12753

In this example, not only did we have the typical price relationships that we look for in a two-step pattern, but we also had another symmetry projection from a prior low-to-high swing that just happened to overlap the other relationships. Also, the swing from point c to point d was only 11 points. Since the difference between a 1.272 extension and a 1.618 extension of an 11-point move was minimal, both the 1.272 and the 1.618 extensions of point c to point d ended up overlapping the other price relationships. It does strengthen a setup when other price relationships also overlap the two-step pattern plan, especially if they are symmetry projections. A decline of 87 points was seen from the high into this two-step pattern cluster.

FIGURE 8-9

Figure 8-9 is a two-step pattern that showed up on a three-minute chart in the mini-sized Dow. A price cluster was formed at the 12762–12764 area. The price relationships were:

.382 retracement of the 12816 high to the 12732 low
(point a to point b) = 12764

1.272 extension of the 12757 high to the 12737 low
(point c to point d) = 12762

1.0 projection of the 12732 low to the 12757 high, projected from the 12737 low (point b to point c, projected from point d) = 12762.

The actual high was made at 12761, just one tick below the cluster zone. This was followed by a pretty quick decline of 38 points.

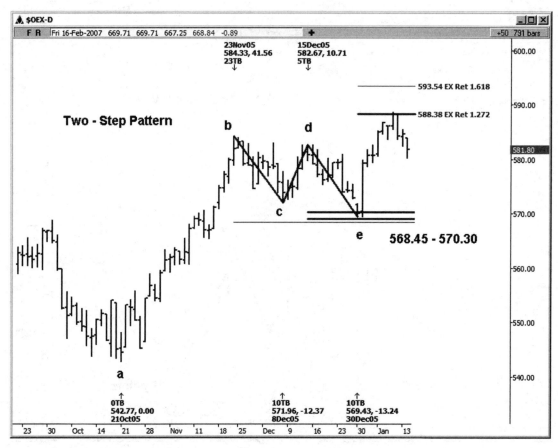

FIGURE 8-10

The next two-step pattern example (see Figure 8-10) is on the daily OEX cash chart. Here we had the coincidence of a .382 retracement from point a to point b, a 1.272 extension of point c to point d, and a 1.0 price projection of point b to point c, projected from point d.

.382 retracement of the 542.77 low to the 584.33 high
(point a to point b) = 568.45

1.272 extension of the 571.96 low to the 582.67 high
(point c to point d) = 569.05

1.0 projection of the 584.33 high to the 571.96 low, projected from the 582.67 high (point b to point c, projected from point d) = 570.30

The actual low was made at 569.43. It was followed by a rally of over 19 points, reaching the initial upside target of the pattern at the 1.272 extension.

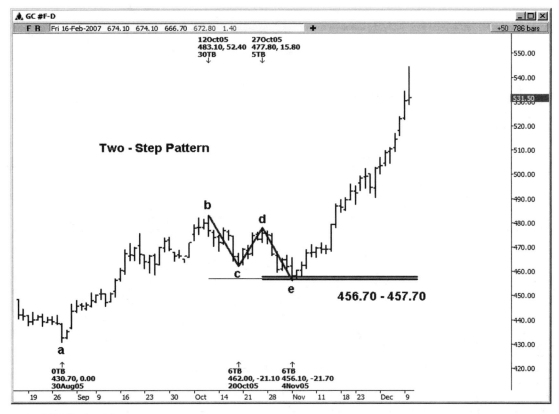

FIGURE 8-11

The next example of a two-step cluster was found on a daily continuous chart in the gold market (see Figure 8-11). It included a 50 percent retracement of point a to point b, a 1.272 extension of point c to point d, and a 1.0 projection of point b to point c, projected from point d. The zone came in between 456.70 and 457.70.

.50 retracement of the 430.70 low to the 483.10 high
   (point a to point b) = 456.90

1.272 extension of the 462.00 low to the 477.80 high
   (point c to point d) = 457.70

1.0 projection of the 483.10 high to the 462.00 low, projected from the
   477.80 high (point b to point c, projected from point d) = 456.70

The low in this case was made at 456.10. This was just a bit below the low end of the cluster at 456.70 (60 cents). Remember not to always expect perfection in this work. An $88 rally followed this low.

141

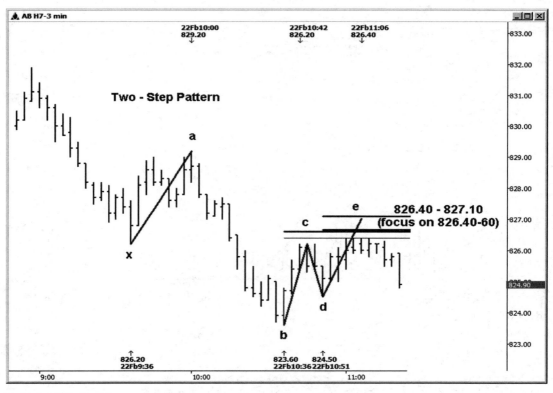

FIGURE 8-12

Not every two-step pattern plays out. As a matter of fact, many of them are violated every day, just like regular price cluster setups, and some of them play out only partially. Let's look at one of those examples where the pattern did not play out fully. This example occurred on a three-minute chart in the E-mini Russell contract (see Figure 8-12). The two-step cluster zone came in at 826.40–827.10, with a focus on the 826.40–826.60 area (three of the price relationships came together within that tighter range).

The price relationships were:

.50 retracement of the 829.20 high to the 823.60 low
(point a to point b) = 826.40

1.272 extension of the 826.20 high to the 824.50 low
(point c to point d) = 826.66

1.0 projection of the 823.60 low to the 826.20 high, projected from the 824.50 low (point b to point c, projected from point d) = 827.10

1.0 projection of the 826.20 low to the 829.20 high, projected from the 823.60 low (point x to point a, projected from point b) = 826.60

FIGURE 8-13

A high was made at the low end of this two-step cluster, and we did start to see a bit of a decline. Figure 8-13, however, illustrates that the pattern never fully played out. After a bit more than a .618 retracement back to the low at 823.60, the rally resumed, rather than heading for the typical downside target at the 822.84 area, which was the 1.272 extension of point b to point e. (Points b and e are illustrated in Figure 8-12.)

> **Author Tip** Sometimes these two-step pattern setups play out in a textbook fashion as far as reaching at least the initial trade target of 1.272 of the whole zigzag. Don't get stuck believing that this is always the case, however. Although many two-step patterns do make the initial target and then some, there are plenty that don't play out fully. For this reason, I recommend using a trailing stop just in case.

FIGURE 8-14

Let's look at an example in the cash Dow $INDU that set up on a 15-minute chart (see Figure 8-14). A two-step pattern and price cluster setup developed at the 12384.20–12396.92 area. It included four key price relationships.

.50 retracement of the 12510.81 high to the 12257.58 low = 12384.20

.618 retracement of the 12470.52 high to the 12257.58 low = 12389.18

1.618 extension of the 12355.23 high to the 12287.78 low = 12396.92

1.0 projection of the 12257.58 low to the 12355.23 high, projected from the 12287.78 low = 12385.43

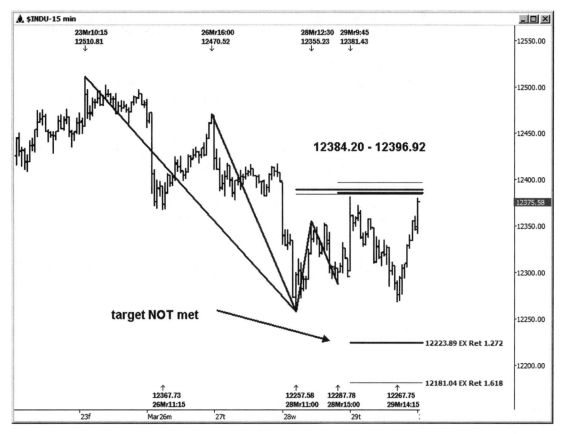

FIGURE 8-15

A high was made just a touch below this two-step cluster at the 12381.43 level, as shown in Figure 8-15. A healthy decline did start from this pattern, but after trading a touch below the .786 retracement back to the 12257.58 swing low, the rally resumed, and the 1.272 target was never met. It was *still* a great trade setup. It just didn't give us the target that we typically look for.

Author Tip If you see a zigzag pattern start to develop on the particular chart you are analyzing, run the price relationships and see if you get the clustering effect. When these setups do play out as planned, they can be rather lucrative.

In this chapter, you learned about the two-step pattern setup, which is sometimes also called a Gartley pattern. This setup, along with the price cluster and symmetry trade setups, offers another trading opportunity with well-defined risk and the potential for some healthy profits.

You now know the basics of how to create a type 1, 2, or 3 trade setup if you have gotten through the first eight chapters of this book. (Note that not all of these trade setups will result in tradable reversals.) Many of these trade setups will be violated or negated. To raise your percentage of winning trades, these setups need to be *filtered* by a good set of indicators and/or price triggers, and ideally should be set up within the direction of the trend. The triggers and indicators that I like to use in my trading plan, along with a few others, will be discussed in a later chapter.

9 CHAPTER

CHOOSING THE SWINGS FOR ANALYSIS

A question that my students always ask is: which highs and lows or price swings do you use to run the analysis from? Beyond learning from the following examples, I'll ask you to use a little bit of common sense. When you are looking at a chart and considering which highs and lows to run the price relationships from, ask yourself whether the results from the highs and lows you are using are relevant to the current market.

CHART EXAMPLES

This first example, Figure 9-1, is on a 15-minute chart in the E-mini Russell. The highs and lows that I would use for both time and price analysis are labeled on the chart. The points I have chosen are all well-defined swing highs and lows that will help me identify my trade setups. I can see in my mind's eye the opportunities for running multiple price retracements, price extensions, and price projections using the highs and lows I have identified on this chart.

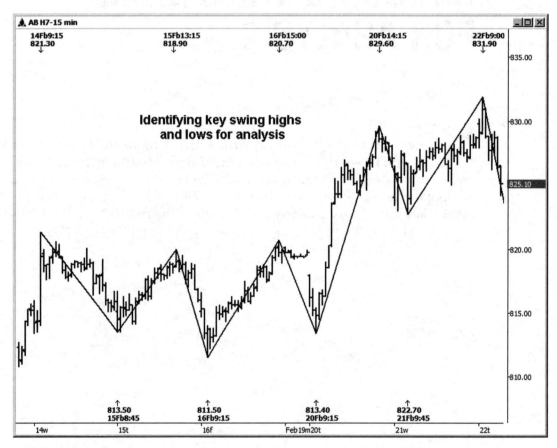

FIGURE 9-1

On the daily euro FX chart (EUR/USD) shown in Figure 9-2, the swings that are obvious to me to use in my analysis are labeled. In this example, I would also use the swing between points a and b as long as it still made sense. For example, projecting symmetry using that swing from the 12/4/06 high made sense until the market declined by more than 100 percent of that prior swing down. At that point, the market would have violated the symmetry support that would have been projected from that swing.

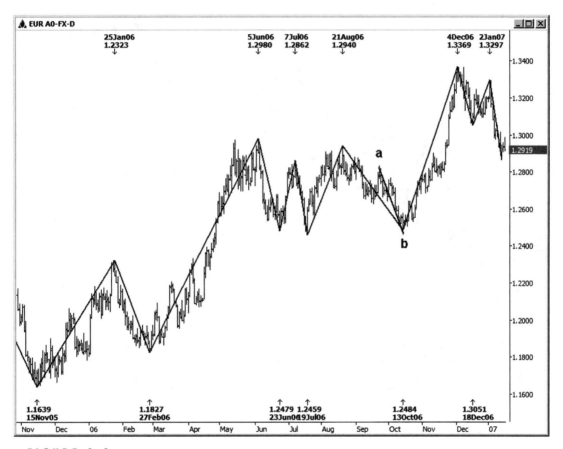

FIGURE 9-2

Figure 9-3 is an example of a daily chart of General Motors (GM). I've labeled the swings I would use for both price and time analysis on this stock.

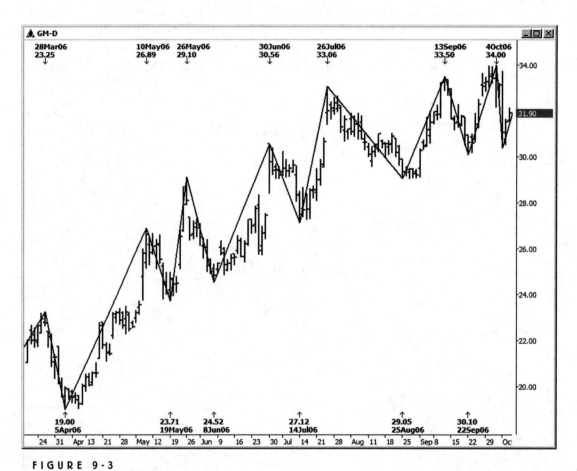

FIGURE 9-3

Figure 9-4 is a daily chart of Google. I've labeled the swings that would make sense for the analysis. To me, the highs and lows to use for analysis are obvious.

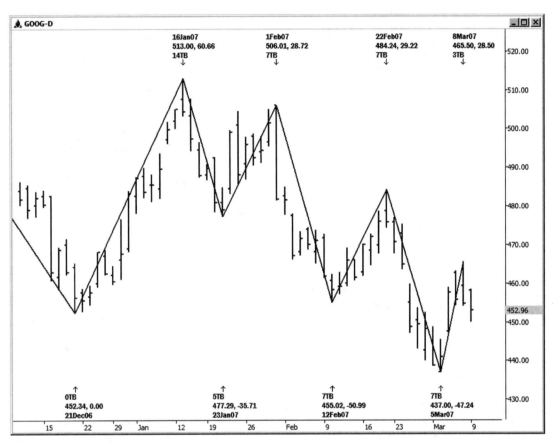

FIGURE 9-4

On the 240-minute euro FX chart (EUR/USD) shown in Figure 9-5, the swings labeled are the ones that stand out for use in both time and price analysis of this chart.

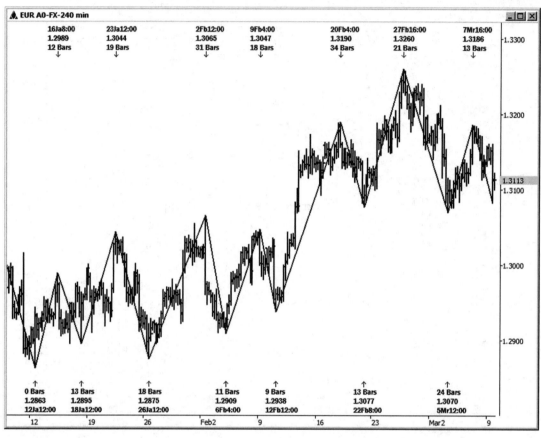

FIGURE 9-5

In Figure 9-6, the swings on the daily "Cable" (GBP/USD) chart that should be used for analysis are labeled on the chart.

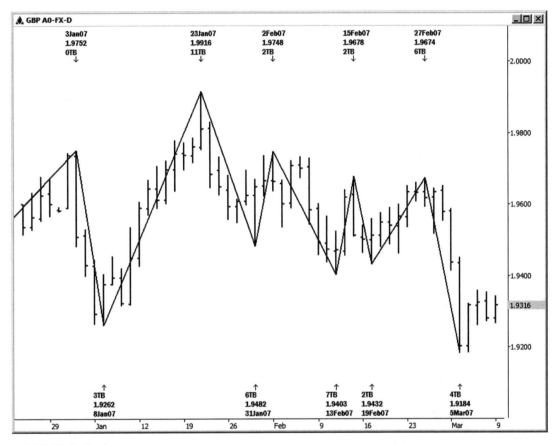

FIGURE 9-6

Figure 9-7 shows a 15-minute chart of the April 2007 mini-sized gold contract. I have labeled the swings that I would have used for my analysis.

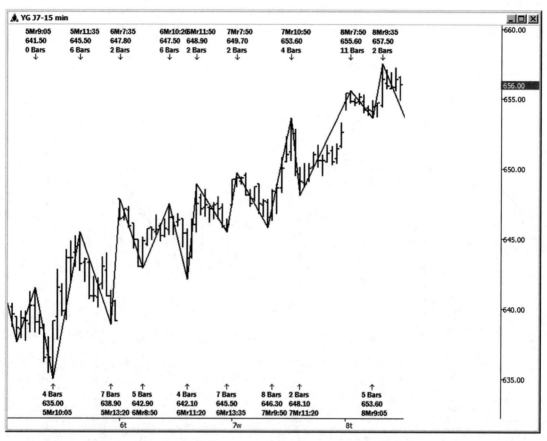

FIGURE 9-7

This chapter was meant to give you a visual guide to the types of swings or highs and lows you should be choosing for your analysis. Once you have a good idea of where to run your price relationships from, with a good analysis program the rest is relatively easy.

You've heard me mention timing or time analysis. Now that we've gone through all the steps to run our price analysis, it is time to focus on *time*. Let's look at how we can apply Fibonacci ratios on the time axis of the market, which can increase the odds of a trade setup playing out if these time cycles coordinate with your price work.

10

C H A P T E R

APPLYING FIBONACCI RATIOS ON THE TIME AXIS OF THE MARKET

A trader can use Fibonacci price analysis and setups as the basis for a very powerful trading plan. To add confirmation and/or strength to these setups, you can apply the same Fibonacci ratios used on the price axis of the market on the time axis as well. Now you are truly *timing* the market, unlike other analysts who say that they are timing the market but are really just referring to using price oscillator reversals. We use these timing cycles to identify time windows in which the market is more likely to reverse. Also, when *time* and *price* parameters come together at the same time, this dramatically raises the odds of a trade setup triggering and playing out.

RUNNING TIME ANALYSIS

There are two ways in which I run my time analysis in the markets. The first way is by running time cycle projections in Dynamic Trader. This Fibonacci timing tool is also available to many traders in their technical analysis packages. Ninja Trader and Genesis Financial have also recently added this tool as an option.

The second way I run my time analysis is with a special report option in the Dynamic Trader program. After I choose the swing highs and lows I want to use to make the time projections, Dynamic Trader automatically takes the same ratios I use in analyzing price and creates a *histogram* below the price chart. This histogram will visually show me a confluence of time projections that we should pay attention to for a possible trend change.

APPLYING TIME CYCLE PROJECTIONS

With Fibonacci time cycle projections, we are looking for a possible trend reversal of whatever the market is doing at the time of the projection(s). For example, if the market is rallying into a .618 time cycle, we would look for a possible high and trend reversal to develop around this cycle, which in this case would suggest that the market will turn back down. Similar to our work with Fibonacci price relationships, we are also looking for a confluence or *clustering* of time relationships to identify a standout time window for a possible change in trend. Single cycles can definitely turn a market, but the odds will always be better when you see a clustering of time cycles. To find these confluences, we will measure the *time* between key swing highs and lows and make projections forward in time, using the same ratios used to analyze the price axis of the market. We will start our analysis with a Fibonacci timing tool that projects from two points on the chart to identify some of these time relationships.

The time relationships that can be projected from two points are the following:

Low to low
High to high
Low to high
High to low

The ratios that I primarily use for timing projections between two points are .382, .50, .618, .786, 1.0, 1.272, 1.618, and 2.618. Occasionally I will use .236 and 4.236 for confirming ratios. By this I mean that they are not that important by themselves, but if they overlap my other time projections, this helps to confirm that those projections are important.

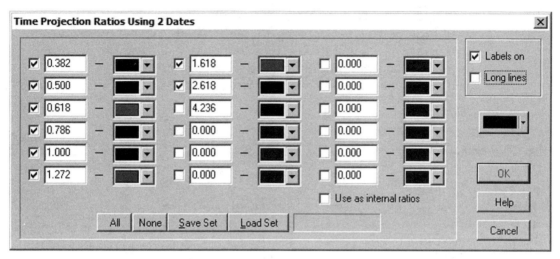

FIGURE 10-1

Figure 10-1 shows you the setup of the time projection tool using two points in the Dynamic Trader software.

Let's review each of the time cycle projections mentioned. Most of the first timing examples are illustrated on a daily continuous chart of the mini-sized crude oil contract. (You will find that I will use quite a few of the mini futures contracts, since many of my clients trade these contracts online.

> **Author Tip**   I use trading days rather than calendar days for projections when running Fibonacci time cycles. However, DT will automatically shift to calendar-day projections when I am using the Dynamic Time reports that will be discussed later. Between trading-day and calendar-day projections, there is typically a difference of a day or two. Personally, I think that trading-day projections tend to be more accurate. It doesn't hurt to run the projections both ways, however, and be aware of the differences in the time projections.

Figure 10-2 is a daily crude chart illustrating an example of how we would run time cycles from a prior high to high. When I use the Dynamic Trader software, I will choose the two points that I want to measure time from, and then the program will project forward from the second point using the same ratios I use in my price analysis, as mentioned earlier.

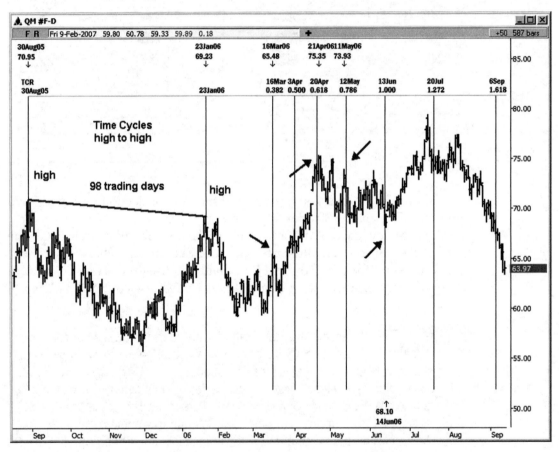

FIGURE 10-2

In this example I chose the 8/30/05 high as the first anchor point on the chart and then chose the 1/23/06 high as the second point. The program measures the distance in time between the two points chosen, which in this case was 98 trading days. The 98 days is then multiplied by the appropriate ratios and projected forward in time. On this chart, you can see some turning points or changes in trend, typically within one trading day of the projected cycles. The March 16 (.382), April 20 (.618), May 12 (.786), and June 13 (1.0) cycles produced a tradable change in trend. The actual dates of the highs or lows were March 16, April 21, May 11, and June 14. Typically we want to watch a time cycle projection plus or minus one day for a possible change in trend. Note that the *other* cycles illustrated in this chart did not produce any meaningful change at all.

Author Tip These are only single-cycle projections that indicated possible changes in trend in advance. When we actually see a *clustering* of these time cycles, the odds for a change in trend or reversal improve dramatically.

Figure 10-3 illustrates time cycles projected from a prior low to low, also illustrated on the daily continuous crude chart. Here we measured the cycle from the 5/16/05 low to the 11/30/05 low, which lasted 137 trading days, and projected the cycles forward from .382 to 1.618. On this chart, we saw reversals near or on .382 in time, .786 in time, 1.272 in time, and 1.618 in time of this prior low-to-low cycle. A low was made one day after the .382 cycle, another low was made exactly on the .786 cycle, a high was made exactly on the 1.272 cycle, and another high was made one day after the 1.618 cycle. (It looks like we also saw a reversal around the 50 percent cycle, but it doesn't look like a clean hit, and I tend to be a perfectionist. I consider it a hit if it is plus or minus one day from the cycle projection.)

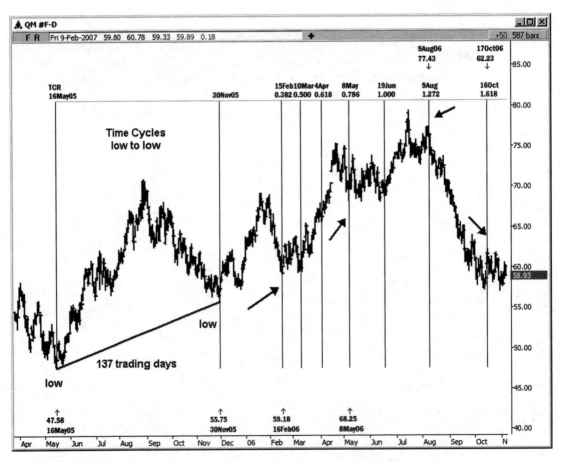

FIGURE 10-3

The next example in the crude oil shows us a high-to-low projection from the 8/30/05 high to the 11/30/05 low swing, which lasted 63 trading days (see Figure 10-4). All the same cycles were projected from this swing. On this chart, we saw a reversal within one trading day of the 1.0 cycle; it came in on a Friday, and the actual high was made on Monday. Another tradable reversal was seen exactly on the day of the 1.618 cycle.

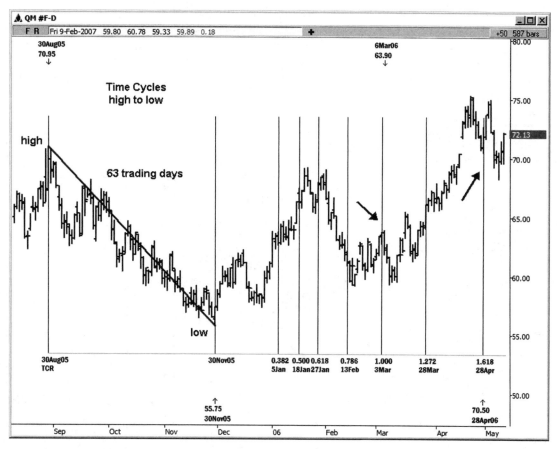

FIGURE 10-4

The next example (see Figure 10-5) illustrates a low-to-high projection from the 11/30/05 low to the 4/21/06 high, using the same Fibonacci ratios as in our prior examples. Here we saw quite a few market reversals develop where the time cycles hit. We saw a low develop at the .382 time cycle. A high developed at the .618 time cycle. Another high developed at .786 in time. A low developed at the 1.272 time cycle, and last but not least, we saw a bit of a reversal right around the 1.618 time cycle!

After running all the possible time cycles with the timing tool that uses two anchor points, we will also use a Fibonacci timing tool that uses three points on the chart where we will compare swings in the same direction in time. It can also be used to compare other disconnected swings. For an example of a disconnected swing, you can measure the distance of a

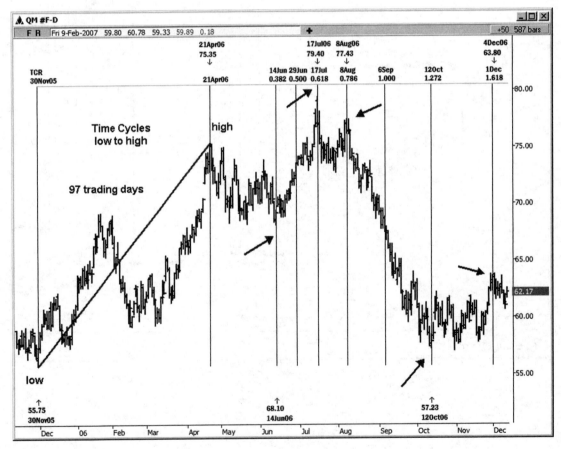

FIGURE 10-5

prior high to high and then project the cycles forward from a swing low in between these two highs.

The time relationships projected using three points that I use most often are the following:

Low to high projected from another low (comparing swings in the same direction)

High to low projected from another high (comparing swings in the same direction)

High to high projected from an intervening low

Low to low projected from an intervening high

For these time projections from three points, I primarily use the ratios 1.0, 1.272, and 1.618. I sometimes use .618 as a confirming ratio here.

Comparing swings in the same direction in time using the 1.0 projection will show you where there is *symmetry* in time. I especially like to run the 100 percent time projections of prior corrective swings to help the trader to enter the market in the direction of the trend. As with symmetry projections on the price axis of the market, we will often see corrective moves terminate at points where there is symmetry in *time* with some prior corrective move.

Figure 10-6 shows the setup of the time projection tool using three points in the Dynamic Trader software.

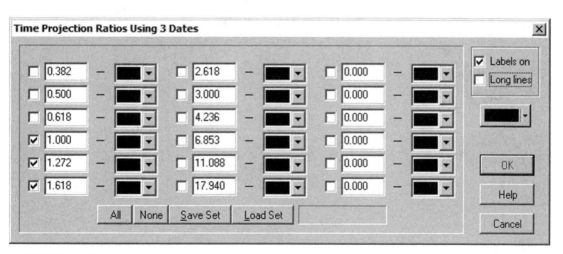

FIGURE 10-6

In the example in Figure 10-7, we are comparing swings in the same direction in time with the time projection tool that uses three anchor points on a chart. My mentor, Robert Miner, calls this an alternate time projection. My first two anchors on this chart are the 2/9/05 low and the 4/4/05 high. These anchors marked a 36-trading-day rally swing. The third anchor on this chart is the 11/30/05 low. This is where we start projecting the cycles from. The cycles we project using the three-point tool are 1.0, 1.272, and 1.618.

The first cycle (1.0) produced a healthy change in trend. The 1.0 cycle came in on 1/24/06. The actual high was made on 1/23/06, just one day prior to the cycle. This is a good example of time symmetry, as the first 36-trading-day swing is similar to the 35-trading-day swing that started in late November. As you begin to study the market on your own, you will

FIGURE 10-7

find that many swings in time will be similar to others in the market you are analyzing.

The next example, Figure 10-8, illustrates a high to low projected from another high. We are again using the three-point timing tool to compare swings in the same direction. Here we took the swing from the 4/4/05 high to the 5/16/05 low, which was a 30-trading-day swing, and then projected the ratios of this swing from the 4/21/06 high. In this case, we saw a reversal develop within a day of the 1.272 cycle, which came due on 6/15/06. The actual low was made on 6/14/06.

FIGURE 10-8

In the next time-cycle example (see Figure 10-9), we are measuring the time of a high-to-high cycle and then projecting the Fibonacci ratios from a key low in between the two highs. The first two anchor points in this example are the 8/30/05 high and the 1/23/06 high, which was a 98-day cycle. We then projected forward from the 11/30/05 low using the ratios 1.0, 1.272, and 1.618. A tradable high was made on 4/21/05, which was one trading day prior to the 4/24/05 cycle. A minor low was made on the 1.272 cycle on 6/1/06. Another tradable high was made within two trading days of the 1.618 cycle. (I usually don't consider that a "hit" in timing, but it is worth being aware of these cycles anyway just in case they do kick in a little late.)

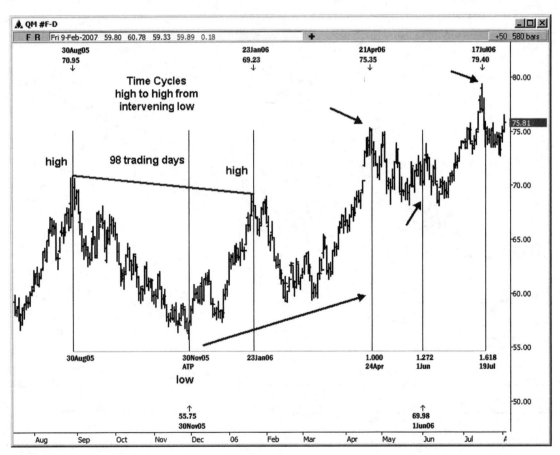

FIGURE 10-9

Figure 10-10 shows a low-to-low cycle with the ratios projected from an intervening high. The low-to-low cycle was from 2/9/05 to 5/16/05 and lasted 66 trading days. The intervening high we projected from was 4/4/05. Again we projected forward in time from the 4/4/05 high using the ratios 1.0, 1.272, and 1.618. Only the 1.0 cycle was worth something in this case. A tradable high was seen on the exact day that cycle hit. Note that the low-to-low swing from the 2/9/05 low to the 5/16/05 low was exactly the same length (66 trading days) as the swing from the 4/4/05 high to the 7/7/05 high.

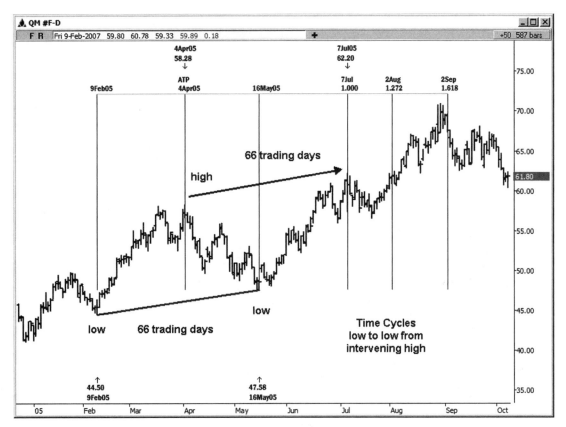

FIGURE 10-10

TIME SYMMETRY

Like price symmetry, time symmetry is a very simple yet powerful trading tool. The following example in Google stock is exactly what we should be looking for in the market. In Figure 10-11, I have labeled three corrective swings that are all similar or equal in time. First we had the swing from the 4/21/06 high to the 5/19/06 low, which lasted 20 trading days. Then we had the swing from the 7/7/06 high to the 8/3/06 low, which was a 19-trading-day swing. The last swing was also a 20-trading-day swing, from the 11/22/06 high to the 12/21/06 low.

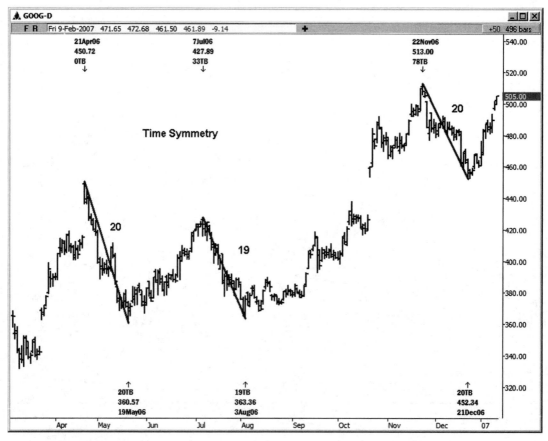

FIGURE 10-11

On this next daily Google chart (Figure 10-12), we'll look at how you could have made some time symmetry projections once you had a prior swing to work with. After this stock rallied from the 5/19/06 low, one of the cycles you could have projected whenever you started to see an extended decline from any new high was 100 percent of the prior decline. In this case, you would have projected the prior 20-trading-day decline from the new high made on 7/7/06. The cycle date came in at 8/4/06, and the actual low was made on 8/3/06, just one trading day before this cycle. Look at the huge rally that followed the 8/3 low! Then from the 11/22/06 high, you would have projected both of the prior declines from that new

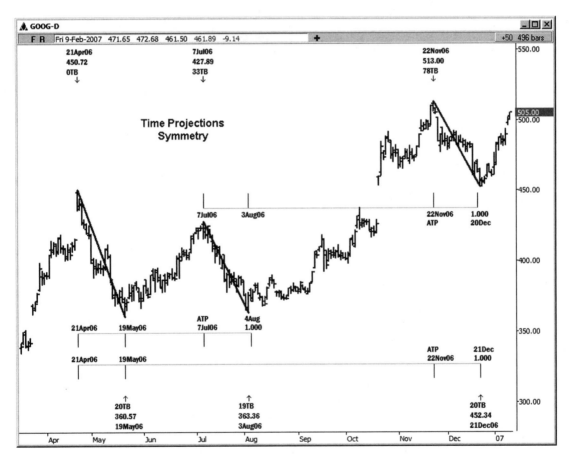

FIGURE 10-12

high. Those projections would have given you two dates, 12/20/06 and 12/21/06, to watch for a possible low. A tradable low was made on 12/21/06 in this case.

These cycles could have been projected from any high where you started to see a market reversal. For example, if we had projected these time cycles from a high that formed before the 11/22 high, the projections for a potential reversal would have been valid at that time. Once a new high was made beyond the high you projected from, however, the projections would have been negated.

Author Tip One thing about this Fibonacci work: every time a new swing high or low is made, there is an opportunity to run new price and time relationships.

Let's take this Google example even further. Timing by itself *can* produce a change in trend in the market, but the higher-probability trade setups are going to occur when both time *and* price parameters come together. As Google was approaching two time projections for a possible low around 12/20–12/21, a price support cluster had developed at the 447.01–452.02 area. If you knew in advance that there was price support along with timing for a low, it is more likely that you would have entered a long position once it was apparent that the price support was holding along with the key timing parameters.

The following Google chart (see Figure 10-13) is a great example of time and price coming together. When time and price parameters align, this is when the odds for a market reversal are even greater than usual.

FIGURE 10-13

In this chapter, I have shown you examples of how to apply Fibonacci ratios on the *time* axis of the market. Note that single time cycles can produce a change in trend by themselves, but the real magic comes into play when you find the time cycles clustering together, similar to what we see with the Fibonacci price cluster relationships. Fibonacci time clusters will be the focus of the next chapter.

11

FIBONACCI TIME CLUSTERS

Now that you know the basic time projections to run for your analysis, you want to look for a coincidence or confluence of at least three of these time relationships within a relatively tight range of time. That is essentially the definition of a time cluster. These cycles will identify a time window for a potential trend reversal—*if* the market is actually trending into it. For example, if the market is rallying into timing, we will look for a possible high and downside reversal to develop as the odds for such a reversal are higher at this time. If the market is declining into timing, we will look for a possible low and upside reversal to develop. Let's talk about what we should consider "a relatively tight range in time" and a "time window" and define them.

With regard to a time range for a cluster, on a daily chart, I will generally look for dates that come within one to three trading days of each other. On an intraday chart, let's call it one to three trading bars on the time frame chart that you are using. Anything much wider than that might not be as useful as far as predictive ability is concerned. I say "might not" be as useful because there are always some exceptions to the rule. Typically, though, the tighter the range of time, the better.

As far as what I mean by a time window, take the time cluster projections and add one bar before them and one bar after them. This creates the time window where you will look for a potential change in trend. So, for example, let's say that we're looking at a cluster of timing cycles that come together between June 2 and June 3 on a daily chart. The time window in which we would look for a possible change in trend will be extended to June 1 through June 4.

TIME CLUSTER EXAMPLES

Let's look at some time cluster examples. Figure 11-1 is a daily chart of Caterpillar. Here we saw a beautiful confluence of time relationships that came in between 10/16/06 and 10/20/06, with the focus of the cycles coming in between 10/17 and 10/19.

1.618 of the 9/6/06 high to the 9/22/06 low = 10/19/06

.50 of the 8/4/06 high to the 9/22/06 low = 10/17/06

1.272 of the 8/4/06 high to the 9/6/06 high = 10/16/06

1.618 of the 7/21/06 low to the 8/24/06 low = 10/19/06

1.0 projection of the 6/8/06 low to the 7/3/06 high, projected from the 9/22/06 low = 10/17/06

1.0 projection of the 6/8/06 low to the 8/14/06 low = 10/18/06

1.0 projection of the 8/24/06 low to the 9/22/06 low = 10/20/06

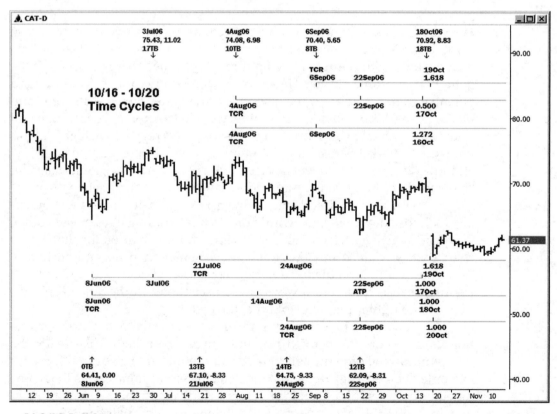

FIGURE 11-1

As CAT was rallying into this cluster of time cycles, we wanted to watch for a possible high to develop, followed by a downside reversal. In this case, the actual high was made on 10/18/06 which was followed by a healthy decline. If I were long this stock, I would certainly want to know that there was time resistance to the rally at that time!

The next time-cycle cluster example, Figure 11-2, is illustrated on a daily chart of GE. From top to bottom, the coinciding cycles were:

1.618 of 10/5/06 high to the 11/2/06 low = 12/19/06

.618 of the 10/5/06 high to the 11/20/06 high = 12/19/06

1.0 projection of the 11/02/06 low to the 11/20/06 high, projected from the 12/1/06 low = 12/19/06

.618 of 11/2/06 low to the 12/1/06 low = 12/19/06

Since GE was trading higher into this grouping of time cycles, we were looking for a possible high to develop. The actual high was made on 12/20/06. When time cycles are due for a possible change in trend in any market, you definitely want to be on alert for any reversal indications or signals.

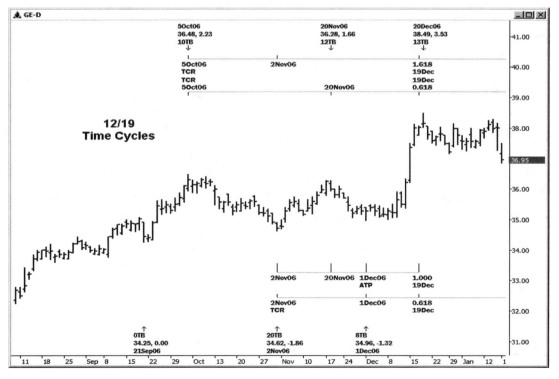

FIGURE 11-2

The gold market has become a fine trading vehicle in recent years. Figure 11-3 illustrates a time cluster that came due between 2/27/07 and 3/1/07. This is something that you would have wanted to be aware of if you had been long gold at that time. The cycles were:

1.0 projection of the 9/5/06 high to the 12/1/06 high = 3/1/07

.618 of the 7/17/06 high to the 12/1/06 high = 2/28/07

1.618 of the 12/1/06 high to the 1/5/07 low = 2/28/07

.618 of the 10/4/06 low to the 1/5/07 low = 3/2/07

1.272 of the 6/14/06 low to the 10/4/06 low = 2/27/07

An intermediate high was made on 2/27/07, which was followed by a $58.00 decline in just over a week.

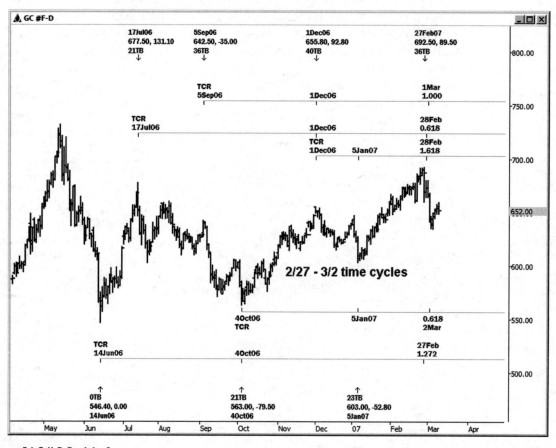

FIGURE 11-3

In MRK stock, we saw a confluence of time cycles between 1/23/07 and 1/25/07 (see Figure 11-4). MRK was rallying into this time window, so we were looking for a possible high to develop in the time window. The cycles were:

1.272 of the 10/27/06 high to the 12/04/06 high = 1/23/07

1.272 of the 12/4/06 high to the 12/26/06 low = 1/25/07

.618 of the 11/10/06 low to the 12/26/06 low = 1/25/07

1.272 projection of the 11/10/06 low to the 12/4/06 high, projected from the 12/26/06 low = 1/25/07

The actual high was made on 1/25/07, which was right on top of the time cycles. A healthy decline was seen from these cycles that lasted for at least 22 trading days. Notice that most of these cycles were projected from only four points on this chart. Many times that is all you will need to find a healthy confluence of cycles. Consider starting your timing work by looking at the most recent key highs and lows.

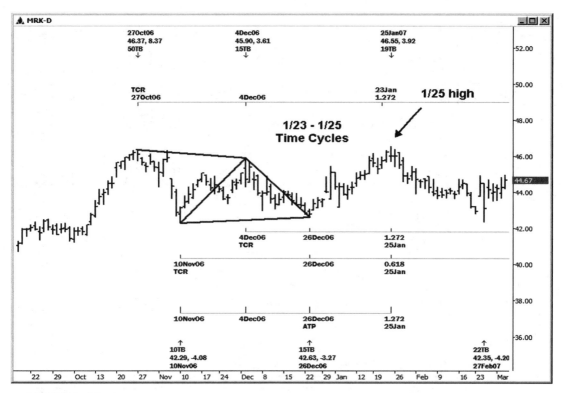

FIGURE 11-4

How about Procter and Gamble (see Figure 11-5)? This stock was also rallying into a time window for a possible high between 11/6/06 and 11/9/06. The coincidence of cycles told us to watch for a possible high to develop.

2.618 of the 10/5/06 high to the 10/16/06 low = 11/9/06
(good confirming cycle)

1.272 of the 9/8/06 high to the 10/5/06 high = 11/8/06

.786 of the period 9/14/06 low to the 10/16/06 low = 11/8/06

1.0 projection of the 9/14/06 low to the 10/5/06 high, projected from the 10/16/06 low = 11/6/06

An intermediate high was made on 11/7/06 and was followed by a tradable decline. Notice the cycle that came due on 11/6/06 at the bottom of the chart. This was an alternate time projection of a prior rally. (This term was coined by my mentor, Robert Miner.) When we are running this type of projection, we are comparing swings in the same direction as far as timing is concerned.

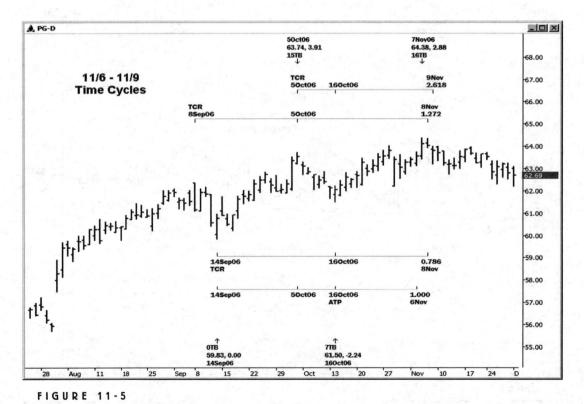

FIGURE 11-5

In this case, I was comparing the prior rally swing, which lasted 15 trading days, to the rally that started at the 10/16/06 low, which ended up lasting 16 trading days. I find these 100 percent time projections rather valuable in timing work. It is essentially symmetry (similarity or equality) on the time axis of these markets.

In Figure 11-6, of PG, besides the time cycles that were illustrated in Figure 11-5, Fibonacci price relationships were also suggesting a possible high at that time. This is due to the overlapping price extensions of two prior swings. In the price work chapters, I mentioned that you should watch for the possible termination of moves at price extensions of prior swings, starting with the 1.272 extension. If you knew that both time and price relationships were coming together in early November, you would have known to protect your profits on any long positions in PG at that time.

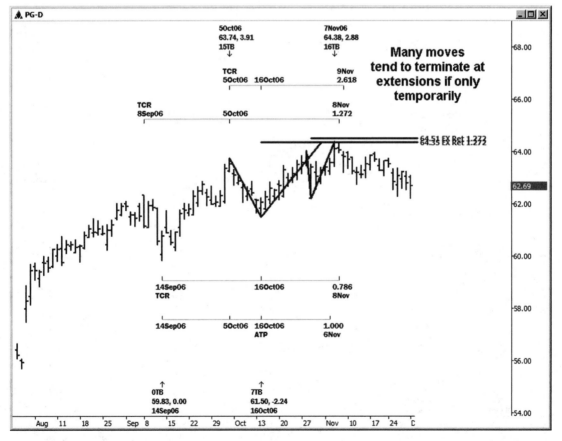

FIGURE 11-6

Figure 11-7, showing the cash Dow Jones Industrial Average, illustrates a healthy time cluster that includes the coincidence of five Fibonacci time relationships between 5/11/04 and 5/14/04. The cycles were:

.618 of the 9/30/03 low to the 2/19/04 high
(point 1 to point 3) = 5/14/04

1.0 of the 11/21/03 low to the 2/19/04 high
(point 2 to point 3) = 5/13/04

1.0 projection of the 2/19/04 high to the 3/24/04 low, projected
from the 4/6/04 high (point 3 to point 4 projected from
point 5) = 5/11/04

2.618 of the 3/24/04 low to the 4/6/04 high
(point 4 to point 5) = 5/11/04

.786 from the 2/19/04 high to the 4/6/04 high
(point 3 to point 5) = 5/13/04

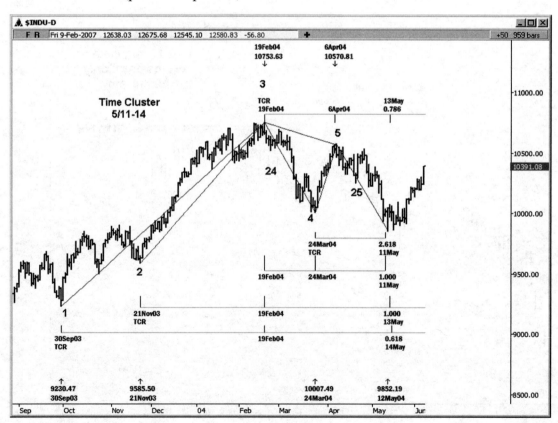

FIGURE 11-7

In the prior chart, it was difficult to fully illustrate two of the cycles listed. The expanded view in Figure 11-8 shows you the full time-cycle projections of the 2.618 cycle of the period from the 3/24/04 low to the 4/6/04 high, and also the time projection from three points, which was the period from the 2/19/04 high to the 3/24/04 low, projected from the 4/6/04 high. Notice the symmetry in time, with the move from point 3 to point 4 being a 24-trading-day decline and the move from point 5 to the actual cycle low made on 5/12 being 25 trading days from the 4/6/04 high.

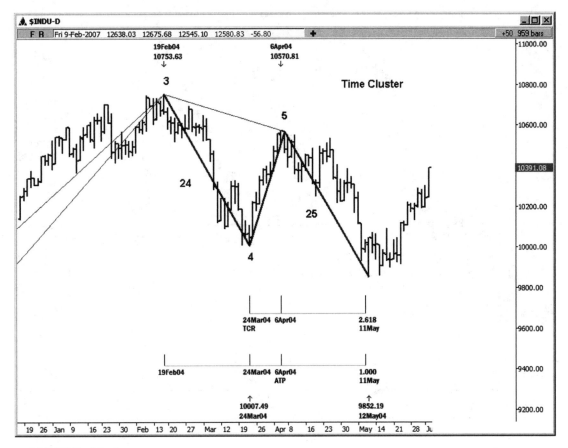

FIGURE 11-8

Figure 11-9 illustrates the price cluster of Fibonacci relationships that coordinated beautifully with this last timing setup on the Dow. As the market was trading down into a key price support zone at the same time that timing parameters were calling for a possible low to develop, you certainly would have wanted to look for reversal signals to the upside. A very healthy rally was eventually seen from the 5/12/04 time and price low.

FIGURE 11-9

Let's look at another time cluster example (see Figure 11-10). This one is illustrated on a daily chart of the cash SPX, where we saw a beautiful confluence of time cycles between 5/9/06 and 5/10/06. Since the market was rallying into the time cycles, we wanted to watch for a possible intermediate high to develop.

The cycles in this cluster were:

1.618 of the 3/21/06 high to the 4/7/06 high = 5/9/06

1.618 of the 4/7/06 high to the 4/20/06 high = 5/9/06
(good confirming cycle)

1.618 of the 1/11/06 high to the 2/27/06 high = 5/9/06

1.0 of the 4/17/06 high to the 4/27/06 low = 5/9/06
(good confirming cycle)

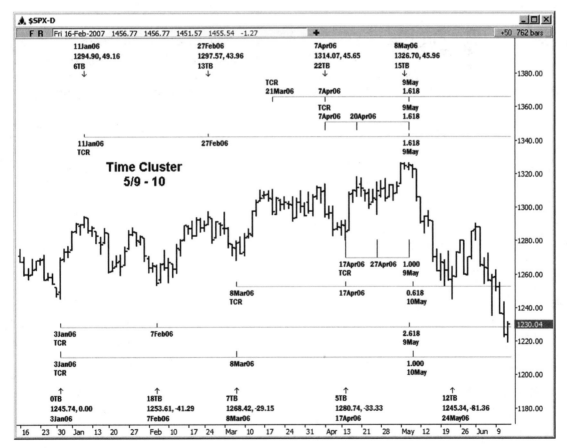

FIGURE 11-10

185

.618 of the 3/8/06 low to the 4/17/06 low = 5/10/06

2.618 of the 1/3/06 low to the 2/7/06 low = 5/9/06
   (good confirming cycle)

1.0 of the 1/3/06 low to the 3/08/06 low = 5/10/06

The actual high in this case was made on 5/8/06, which was one trading day prior to the cycles. This is considered to be within the time window for a high. A rather dramatic decline was seen from this grouping of time cycles.

I listed a few of the cycles as confirming cycles. These cycles are not as important by themselves for a couple of reasons. The 2.618 cycle I always consider a confirming cycle. The other cycles listed are projected from smaller time periods. Relative to the cycles that were projected from the larger time periods, they would tend to be less important.

> **Author Tip** Price work by itself can definitely give you a "heads up" as to when a market move might terminate. Add timing to this mix and the odds for a possible reversal increase dramatically. Why use only one dimension of the market when you can use both the price axis and the time axis?

In this next example, we are looking at another daily chart of the cash SPX index (see Figure 11-11). This timing information was available to my clients before the actual high was made. We were looking at the coincidence of at least four cycles between 2/22/07 and 2/23/07. These cycles are listed below.

1.272 of the 1/25/07 high to the 2/7/07 high = 2/23/07

1.272 of the 1/3/07 high to the 1/25/07 high = 2/22/07

.618 of the 1/26/07 low to the 2/12/07 low = 2/22/07

1.0 projection of the 1/26/07 low to the 2/07/07 high, projected from the 2/12/07 low = 2/23/07

A major high was made on 2/22/07 at 1461.57. This high was made just slightly beyond the 1.272 price extension of the move from the 2/7/07

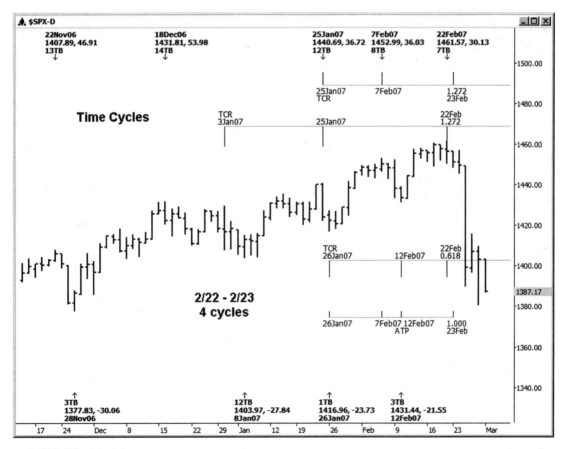

FIGURE 11-11

high to the 2/12/07 low. Between the price and time parameters, we were on alert for the possible termination of the rally and for an intermediate high to develop at that time. This is information that you would certainly want to be aware of if you were long at that time!

Figure 11-12 gives you a preview of how these timing cycles can also be projected with the timing module in the Dynamic Trader software. (This technique will be covered in the next chapter.) With the same daily cash S&P chart we used in the last analysis, I let the Dynamic Time Projection routine run from two of the prior lows on this chart. Both of these time projections showed a time cluster right around 2/22 and 2/23. Sometimes it's nice to have the visual of the time cycle cluster right below the chart. As also illustrated in the last example, the high was made on 2/22, and at the time we took a snapshot of this chart, the S&P had already declined just over 80 full S&P points.

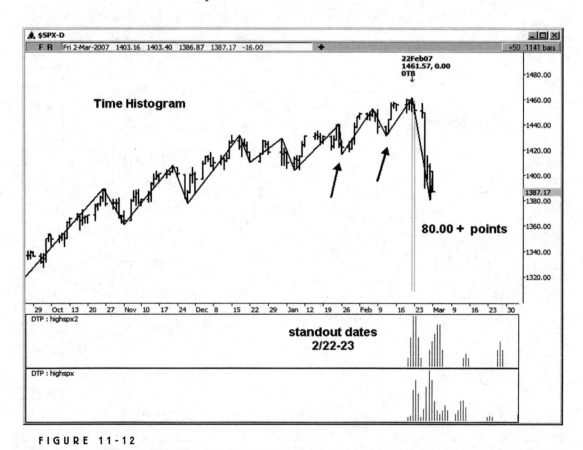

FIGURE 11-12

188

Google is always a fun stock to analyze (see Figure 11-13). We are looking at a daily chart of this stock with a confluence of five Fibonacci time relationships that came due between 2/22/07 and 2/23/07. I have numbered the highs and lows in this example so that it's a little bit easier for you to follow along. All the key highs and lows are also labeled.

1.0 of the 2/1/07 high to the 2/12/07 low
(point 3 to point 4) = 2/22/07
1.272 of the 1/16/07 high to the 2/1/07 high
(point 1 to point 3) = 2/23/07
.382 of the 1/16/07 high to the 2/12/07 low
(point 1 to point 4) = 2/22/07

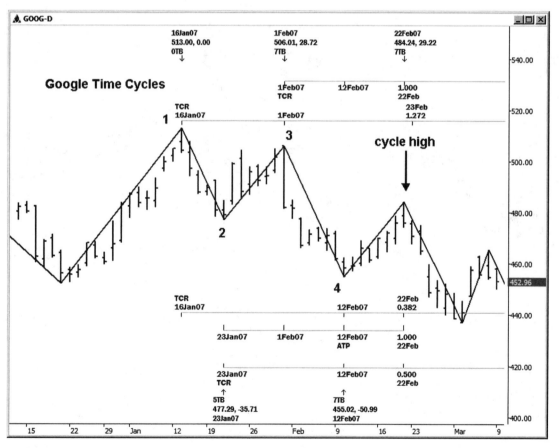

FIGURE 11-13

1.0 projection of the 1/23/07 low to the 2/1/07 high, projected from the 2/12/07 low (point 2 to point 3, projected from point 4) = 2/22/07

.50 of the 1/23/07 low to the 2/12/07 low (point 2 to point 4) = 2/22/07 (good confirming cycle)

I typically do not consider a 50 percent time cycle to be powerful by itself, although I do like it as a confirming cycle. A high was made directly into this time window on 2/22/07.

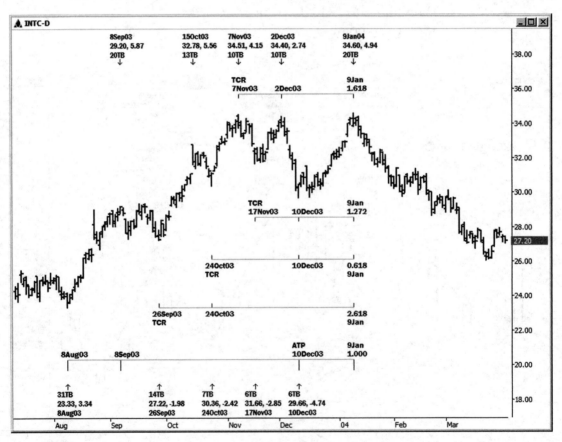

FIGURE 11-14

On the daily chart of Intel stock in Figure 11-14, we saw a beautiful cluster of time cycles that *all* came in on January 9, 2004. From top to bottom of the chart, the cycles were:

1.618 of the 11/7/03 high to the 12/2/03 high = 1/9/04

1.272 of the 11/17/03 low to the 12/10/03 low = 1/9/04

.618 of the 10/24/03 low to the 12/10/03 low = 1/9/04

2.618 of the 9/26/03 low to the 10/24/03 low = 1/9/04
    (good confirming cycle)

1.0 projection of the 8/8/03 low to the 9/8/03 high, projected from the 12/10/03 low = 1/9/04

The actual high in this case was made on 1/9/04. This high was followed by a relatively healthy decline. If you were long INTC into January 9, this is certainly a piece of information that you would have wanted to be aware of.

Fibonacci time clusters are a very powerful trading tool that you can add to your trader's toolbox. Even though Fibonacci price work by itself can be used as a winning trading methodology, the illustrations in this chapter should give you an idea of how you can sharpen your trader's edge in these markets even further by using Fibonacci time cycles. In the next chapter, we will focus on the Fibonacci time histograms that I use on my intraday charts every day in my chat room.

12 CHAPTER

USING DYNAMIC TRADER TIME PROJECTION REPORTS AND HISTOGRAMS

During the trading day, since I am updating about 16 charts down to the 3-minute time frame, I don't really have the time to run individual time cycles down to a 15-minute chart using the time-cycle tool. This is why I use the timing reports within the Dynamic Trader software. After I create a swing file to identify the key swing highs and lows that I want to use in the timing analysis, I will run a timing report from either the last high or the last low on the chart to project times for the next possible low or high to develop. The program will produce a histogram below the chart that will visually show me where there is a clustering of time cycles. When I see a standout in the histogram, I know to prepare for a possible trend reversal if the market I am analyzing is trending into the time cycles indicated by the histogram. This is when I will look for trend reversal signals. If I see any reversal indications, then I have reason to both exit any current positions and, in some cases, look to reverse positions.

Let's look at a few examples using the Dynamic Time Projection report in the DT software. In order to run one of these reports you have to make sure that you have identified the key swing highs and lows by creating a swing file within the DT program. As long as that is done, all you will need to do is place a program marker on the low or high that you want to project forward from, and then run the report. If you are projecting from the last low, you will be looking for a possible high to develop around any time clusters that stand out in the histogram. If you are projecting from the last high, you will be looking for a possible low to develop around any time clusters that stand out on the histogram.

Author Tip   Note that many of these time clusters will *not* produce a change in trend at all, just as not all price cluster zones will hold or produce a change in trend. One thing to be aware of, however, is that if a market trends into a time cluster and it coordinates with price parameters, the odds of making a reversal are higher than when you are seeing only the time relationships by themselves.

In Figure 12-1, we are looking at a 15-minute chart in the E-mini Russell contract. Using the program, I have created a swing file defining the key highs and lows that I feel will be valuable in our time analysis. In this example, I am getting ready to project the time cycles from the last low on this chart, made at 813.50.

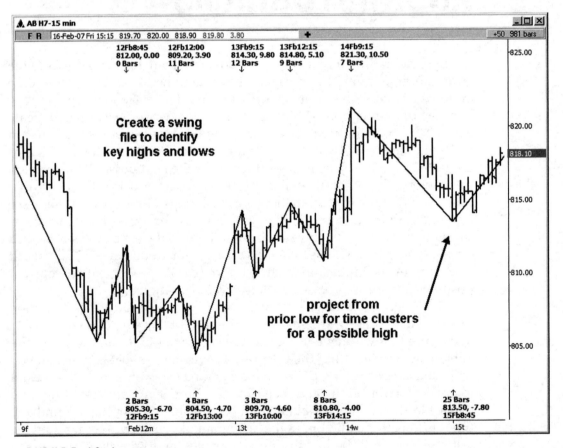

FIGURE 12-1

194

In Figure 12-2, you can see the histogram that was generated by the time projection report. There are two separate standout clusters of cycles that were coming due for a possible high. An actual high and reversal were seen into the first time cluster illustrated on the chart. After the market started to decline from that new high, made at 820.00, I would have run a new time projection report from the 820.00 high to identify time periods where we were more likely to make a low and reversal back to the upside. As a market makes new swing highs and lows, new projections are made to help identify the next time windows for possible market reversal.

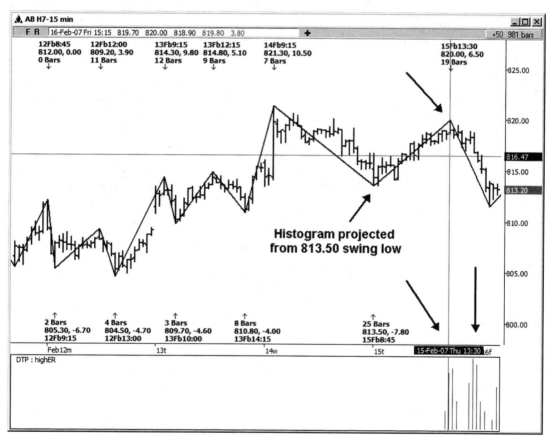

FIGURE 12-2

In Figure 12-3, we are looking at a timing example on a daily chart of Google stock. The general trend of this stock was up. Once we started to see a countertrend decline, we would want to look for both time and price parameters to help us to reenter Google in the direction of the larger trend. Projecting the time-cycle report from the 11/22/06 high would have been helpful in pointing out a time window where the odds for a possible low to develop were higher. The 12/18/06–12/21/06 dates showed up on the histogram, with 12/19/06 as the highest bar within the histogram. The actual low was made on 12/21/06 at 452.34. You may recognize this example from another chart example analyzed earlier using the time-cycle tool. Either way, timing was definitely helpful in identifying a time window for a possible low and reversal to develop in Google. As illustrated in our earlier example, this low was followed by a healthy rally.

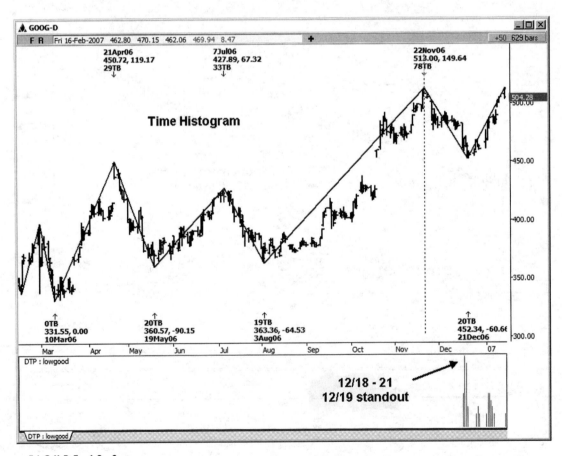

FIGURE 12-3

196

In Figure 12-4, we are looking at a time projection report that was run on the S&P daily cash chart. Here we projected from the 10/26/06 high, looking for a possible low. As you can see on the histogram below the chart, there was a standout projection that came in on 11/05/06, which was a Sunday. The actual low was made on the Friday just prior to the standout cycle. The initial rally from that cycle low was more than 46 full points.

Remember that the time projection report defaults to calendar day projections. For this reason, the timing cycles can show up on a weekend or nontrading day.

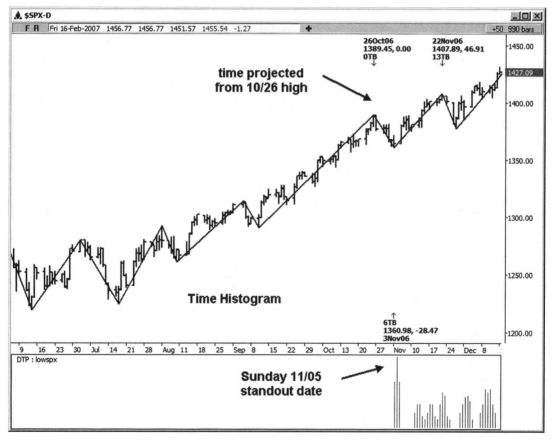

FIGURE 12-4

Figure 12-5 is another example using the same daily S&P cash index, but this time projecting for a possible high from the 11/28/06 low. One of the standouts on the time histogram came in between 12/15/06 and 12/18/06. This was a time when we would have looked for a possible termination of the rally that started from that last low on 11/28/06. An intermediate high was made on 12/18/06. It was followed by a tradable corrective decline.

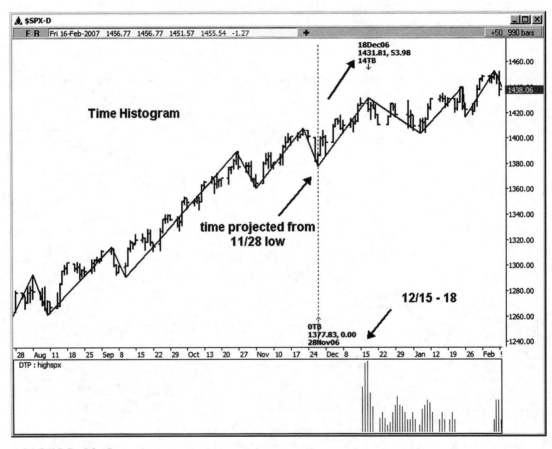

FIGURE 12-5

Figure 12-6 is a daily chart of Intel stock. Here I ran the time projection from the 10/16/06 high, looking for a possible low. Friday, 11/3/06, stood out on the time histogram for a possible low. A tradable low was made on Monday, November 6, which was just one trading day after the standout date on the histogram. This low was followed by a rally of $2.18.

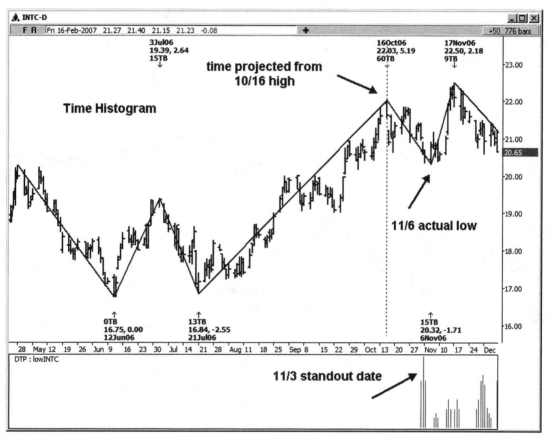

FIGURE 12-6

Let's look at an example on a 15-minute chart in the E-mini Russell. In Figure 12-7, I have run the timing report from the low made at 822.70, looking for time resistance to the rally from that low and a possible high and reversal. You will notice that there are two standout clusters on the histogram below the chart. The first one pretty much nailed the high. A decline of $8.30 followed that timing high.

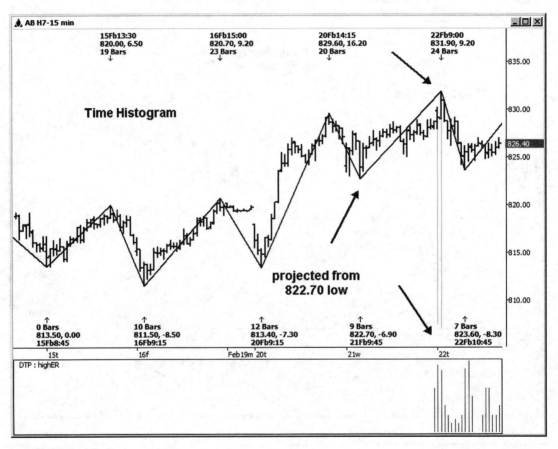

FIGURE 12-7

Figure 12-8 shows the March 2007 mini-sized Dow contract on a 15-minute chart. Notice the standout on the histogram below this chart. When I see an unusually high spike relative to the other time cycles on the histogram, I really want to pay attention to the market at that time. In this example, an important high was made within one bar of the standout on this 15-minute chart. (If you were trading the countertrend rally from the 2/23/07 low, this would have given you the proper warning that the rally might soon terminate!)

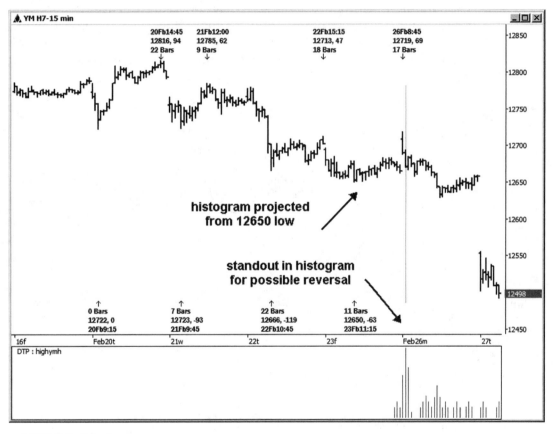

FIGURE 12-8

Author Tip Over the years, I have told my traders that this trading method-ology can be applied on *any* time frame. For example, I have seen perfectly formed two-step patterns or symmetry setups on a one-minute chart and even on a tick chart. As far as timing is concerned, what is the lowest time frame that you would want to run your timing work on? Personally, I don't go lower than a 15-minute chart except "for kicks" every once in a while.

This next example is a "for kicks" example on a five-minute chart of the e-mini Russell contract. Figure 12-9 shows that a low was made within one five-minute bar of the standout on the histogram. I suppose someone could run these cycles on this time frame if he or she were updating only a couple of charts during the trading session. Much more than that would make it difficult to keep up.

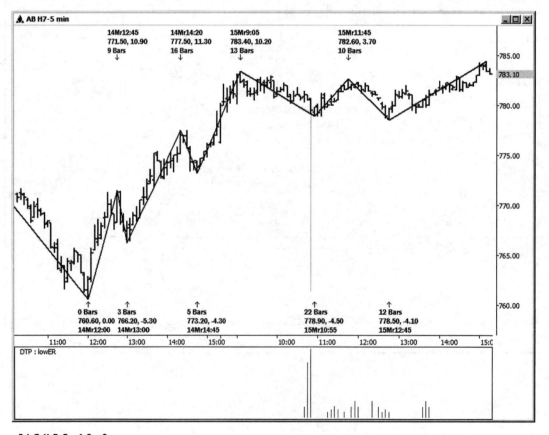

FIGURE 12-9

NUANCES OF TIMING WORK

Whether you choose to run time-cycle projections as illustrated in Chapter 11 or to use the Dynamic Trader histograms for time clusters, you need to understand some of the nuances of timing work. Do not assume that you will see a market reversal just because there is a healthy cluster of time cycles. Time clusters are violated the same way price clusters are violated. If you don't see price reversal indications as you move into a time window for a possible reversal, the market should just continue in the direction of the trend. However, if you do start to see reversal indications, you can jump on the market, knowing that the odds as far as timing goes are on your side.

If the market is going sideways into timing cycles, the predictive value of the time cluster is pretty much lost. One thing that I've observed about a sideways move into a time cluster, however, is that the "energy" of the cycles/projections may bring the market out of the sideways move and get it trending again.

If your time analysis agrees with what your price analysis is showing, the timing work has higher odds of producing a tradable change in trend. For example, if timing is calling for a high and you are at price extensions of the prior swing where trends tend to terminate, this strengthens the predictive value of the timing work. Another example of your price work supporting your timing work would be where you are meeting a price cluster of support or resistance along with the timing.

When choosing the points to run the time projections from, there is one thing you have to consider: there needs to be ample time in between the dates you are running the projections from. For example, if you are running a high-to-high projection where the time elapsed between the highs is 100 trading days, you can easily run all the time projections discussed earlier. If the time in the high-to-high cycle is only 10 trading days, however, running these projections won't have much value, since a cycle will hit at almost every other bar. In cases like this where the swings in time are not very large, you can do a couple of things. First, you can drop down to a lower time frame chart. For example, if the daily chart doesn't seem appropriate for the time analysis, go down to a 60-minute chart, which will display more time bars between the swings. Your other option would be to continue doing the analysis on the daily chart, but to use only the most important cycles. For me, those would be .618, 1.0, and 1.618. This work will take a little bit of common sense. As you work with applying the cycles, in time you will learn what makes sense.

Timing can be run on any *time* frame chart. The question becomes, however, what is *practical*? In my chat room, I typically run the daily time projections and then run 45- and/or 15-minute timing charts to help fine-tune intraday trade entries. Although I have done some work on some charts lower than the 15-minute time frame, it is generally not practical to keep them up on the time frames less than 15 minutes. You would be so busy running the time projections that you would probably miss taking your trade setups!

Author Tip You cannot do accurate timing work with either tick or volume charts, since the time within each of those bars will *not* be equal.

If you plan on doing timing work on an intraday chart, if at all possible, choose a time frame chart that will divide equally or pretty close to equally into the trading session. For examples, there are 405 minutes in the day session in the indexes, from 8:30 a.m. central time to 3:15 p.m. central time. As long as I am analyzing only day-session data, I can divide that 405 minutes into 3 bars with a 135-minute chart, or I can divide it into 9 bars with a 45-minute chart, or into 27 bars with a 15-minute chart. These time charts all divide perfectly into the 405-minute session. If the time period you use doesn't divide well into the session hours, the timing results on your intraday work could be compromised by a discrepancy in the last bar of the day.

In the last few chapters, I've covered using Fibonacci analysis on the time axis of the market using Fibonacci time cycles, which can be found in quite a few market analysis programs, along with the more automated reports that can be projected using the Dynamic Trader software. However, while many charting packages do allow you to project these time cycles from two points, there are only a few that will allow you to run the time projections from three points. The automated time histogram reports that I have discussed in this chapter are only available within the Dynamic Trader program.

13 CHAPTER

TIME AND PRICE
CONFLUENCE

You can use Fibonacci price analysis by itself and create a winning trading plan for yourself. Adding the time element to your market analysis, however, can definitely *increase* your odds for success. I highly recommend that you at least run timing work on your daily charts and let the market prove the value of this technique rather than just taking my word for it! The added dimension of the *time* axis of the market can sometimes make a huge difference in your bottom line. Timing can alert you to tighten stops on current positions and help you hold on to your winnings. Timing will also help you identify excellent entry opportunities when it aligns with price. When you see time and price come together on any time frame, the odds for a change in trend or reversal are much higher. Using a trade entry trigger will raise your odds for success even further. Let's go over some examples of time and price coming together; then we will move on to trade triggers and indicators.

TIME AND PRICE EXAMPLES

In this first example of time and price coming together, we are looking at a daily chart of Google (see Figure 13-1). Here we had a confluence of the timing cycles due between 12/29/05 and 12/30/05 as we tested a key price support cluster at the 414.05–415.61 area. With the elements of both *time* and *price* relationships coming together, we wanted to watch for a possible low and upside reversal to develop at that time. The actual low in this case was made just slightly below the low end of the cluster zone at the 413.74 level. A rally of at least $61.00 was seen relatively quickly from this time/price low.

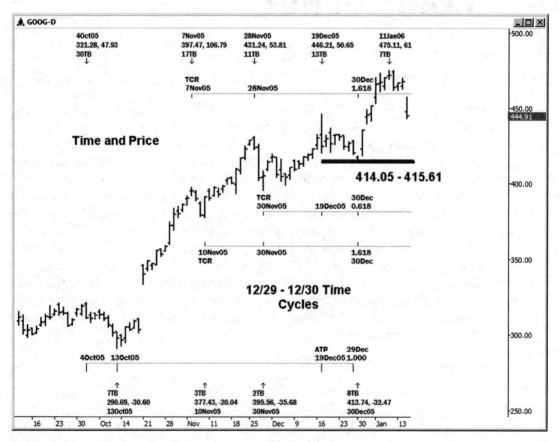

FIGURE 13-1

Let's look at an example of time and price parameters coming together in the mini-sized gold contract traded at the CBOT (see Figure 13-2). Here we are looking at an example on a 15-minute chart. Notice that as gold was trading down from the 657.50 high made on 3/8, there were a few stand-out bars on the timing histogram below the chart. This occurred at the *same* time that a key price support decision was tested at the 651.60–652.20 area. A low was made at 652.10 into these key time and price parameters. This low was followed by a tradable rally.

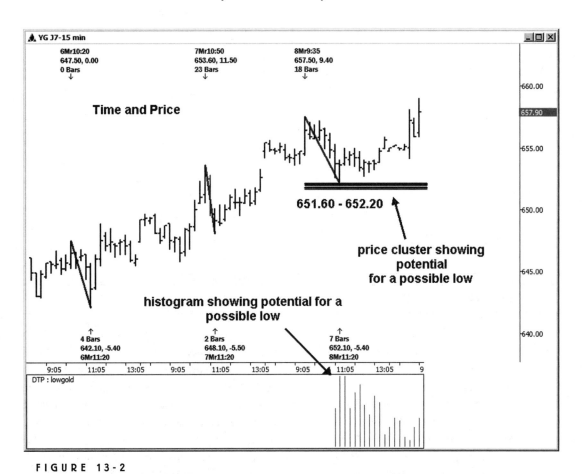

FIGURE 13-2

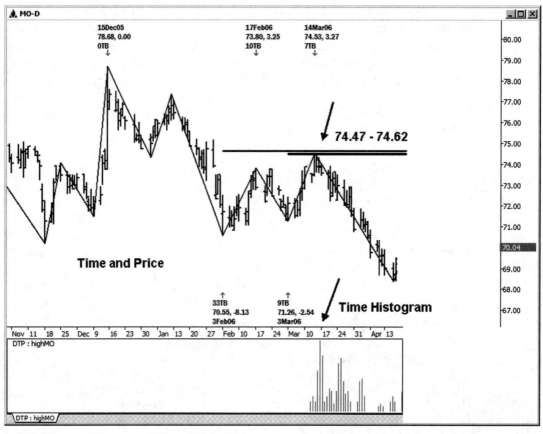

FIGURE 13-3

Depending on my time constraints when I'm running my analysis on any market, I might run a time histogram rather than running the actual time cycles, which is generally more time consuming. In this next example of time and price coming together, I've run it both ways. In the first MO chart, Figure 13-3, you can see a standout bar on the time histogram, which was run from a prior low made on 3/3/06. This histogram was projecting a possible high, since we ran it from the last low as the market was rallying. You can see how the standout bar coincided beautifully with a two-step pattern and price cluster at the 74.47–74.62 area. The actual high was made at 74.53. A healthy decline followed this well-defined time and price coincidence, or, as I like to call it, *synchronicity*. A quick definition of synchronicity is "meaningful coincidence."

Author Tip When I see a meaningful coincidence of time and price parameters, I look for a possible change in trend.

Figure 13-4 illustrates the same trade setup, but it shows the actual time cycles that are represented by the histogram below the chart in Figure 13-3.

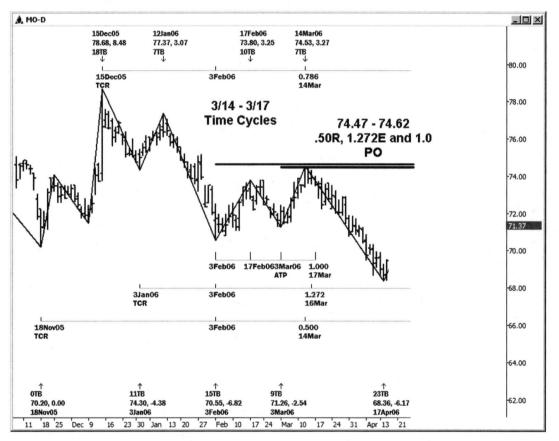

FIGURE 13-4

Figure 13-5 shows that not only did we have timing for a possible high in Google between 2/22/07 and 2/23/07, as illustrated in Chapter 11, but we also had a beautiful price cluster that was tested at the same time. The cluster came in between 483.74 and 486.53. This is a great example of time and price coming together that increases the odds for a market reversal. Google made a high at 484.24 and at the time this chart was prepared had declined by $45. (Knowing where the time and price parameters were on this stock would have prepared you nicely for a short in this stock.)

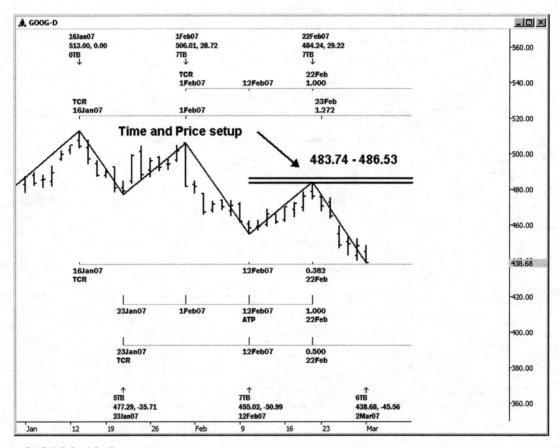

FIGURE 13-5

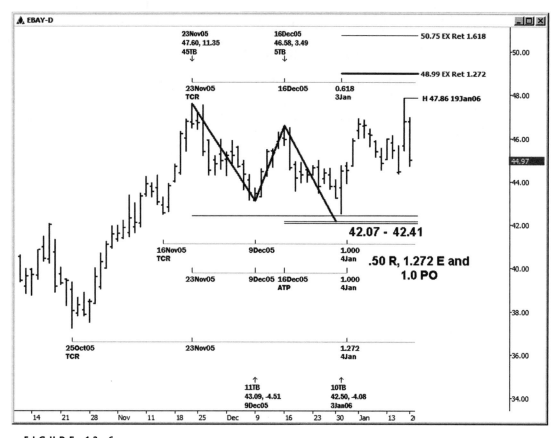

FIGURE 13-6

In eBay we have a nice example of time and price coming together, with a two-step pattern into timing (see Figure 13-6). The zigzag pattern created a price cluster in the 42.07–42.41 area. The cluster included a 50 percent retracement of the move from the 10/25/05 low to the 11/23/05 high, a 1.272 extension of the move from the 12/9/05 low to the 12/16/05 high, and the 100 percent projection of the swing from the 11/23/05 high to the 12/9/05 low, projected from the 12/16/05 high.

As far as timing was concerned, we had four cycles come in between 1/3/06 and 1/4/06:

618 from the 11/23/05 high to the 12/16/05 high = 1/3/06
1.0 from the 11/16/05 low to the 12/9/05 low = 1/4/06

1.0 from the 11/23/05 high to the 12/9/05 low, projected from the 12/16/05 high = 1/4/06

1.272 from the 10/25/05 low to the 11/23/05 high = 1/4/06

The actual low in this case was made at 42.50 on 1/3/06. This was just cents above the key price support cluster. The initial upside target at the 48.99 level was not met, however, we did at least see a rally from this 42.50 low to 47.86.

Google is a stock that seems to respect market geometry more often than not. Figure 13-7 is an example in which time and price came together to produce a tradable low on 3/5/07. On the daily GOOG chart, we can see the coincidence of three price relationships in the 433.25–436.96 area. This included a 1.618 extension of the move from the 2/12/07 low to the 2/22/07 high, a 1.272 extension of the move from the 12/21/06 low to the 1/16/07 high, and a 100 percent price projection of the swing from the 2/1/07 high to the 2/12/07 low, projected from the 2/22/07 high. The time histogram below the chart shows a confluence of timing cycles that came due as this key price support zone was tested. The low was made on 3/5/07 at the 437.00 level (just 4 cents above the high end of the zone) and was followed by an immediate rally of $28.50 into the 3/8/07 high. Also notice that after a retest of the 3/5/07 low, we saw another rally develop.

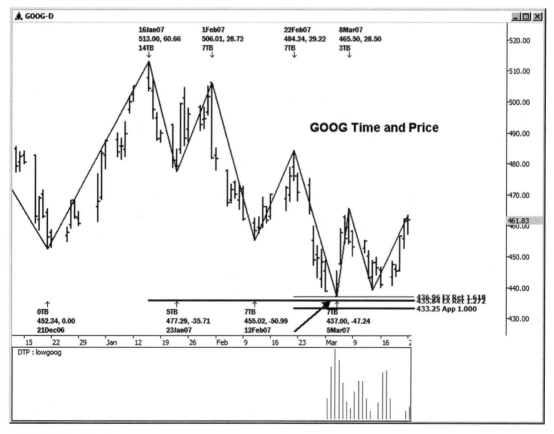

FIGURE 13-7

Figure 13-8 illustrates one of the most important cycles that would have been included in the time histogram of the prior chart. It was the 100 percent cycle of the swing from the 2/1/07 high to the 2/12/07 low, which lasted seven trading days. This was projected from the 2/22/07 high. Note that the 3/5/07 low was made exactly seven trading days from the 2/22/07 high. This is another good example of time symmetry.

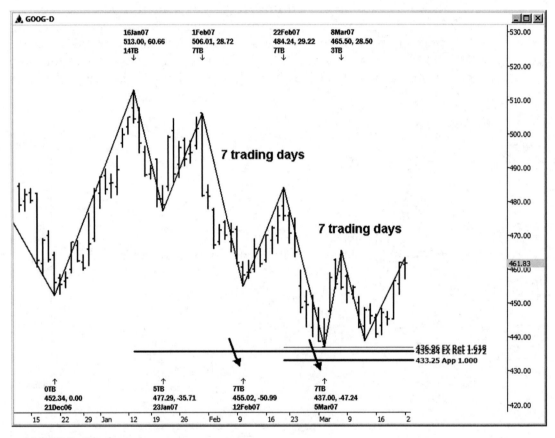

FIGURE 13-8

> **Author Tip** When we talk about time and price coming together, it doesn't always have to be a price cluster setup with a time cluster setup. We could be talking about symmetry in price and time. The bottom line is: as long as we have a key price decision that meets with a key time decision, we can call that time and price coming together, and this is when we watch for a possible market reversal.

A good example of time and price symmetry is illustrated in this next example in Nike stock (see Figure 13-9). With the general trend in NKE down at the time, you would have wanted to watch for a sell setup to develop in order to enter this stock in the direction of the down trend. Here we had a symmetry projection of a prior rally swing from the 1/30/06 low

F I G U R E   1 3 - 9

to the 3/6/06 high, a swing of $7.44. This $7.44 was then projected from the low made on 5/22/06, which suggested possible resistance around the 84.83 area. This was not a perfect hit, as the actual high was made 14 cents above the projection.

At the same time that NKE was approaching resistance, there was symmetry in *time* that was pretty obvious. The prior rally swing had lasted 24 trading days. As this stock rallied into the area of price resistance of the same swing, it had rallied for 23 trading days. With these time and price parameters coming together, a tradable high was seen at 84.97 on 6/23/06. A decline of $9.45 from this time and price high was eventually seen.

The examples in this chapter illustrate how the confluence of time and price relationships can further define important decision points in whatever market you are analyzing. When both the time and price dimensions of the market come together, the odds for a successful trade setup playing out increase dramatically.

14

TRIGGERS AND INDICATORS

In an earlier chapter, I mentioned that many trade setups will be violated. In other words, the market often will not hold *above* the price level or zone of one of the buy setups defined in Chapters 6 through 8, or not hold below the price level or zone of one of the sell setups defined in those same chapters. We know that these trade setups are important market decisions; however, we don't know in advance whether or not a particular zone will hold. To *increase* the odds for success in trading using these trade setups, we ideally want to use *trade filters* and/or a *trade trigger.*

A trade trigger is typically made up of a technical indicator, a price pattern, or a combination of the two. It is what tells us to take *action* or *entry* against a trade setup.

Author Tip	What is good about using a trade trigger is that many of the trade setups that are going to be violated *never* trigger. Of course, we will get some of the setups that do trigger, but eventually fail and result in a loss, but using a trigger will filter out quite a few of those setups.

POTENTIAL TRADE TRIGGERS

A number of different methods can be used as trade triggers.

Taking Out a Prior Swing High or Low

This is a relatively simple entry trigger. The violation of a prior swing high or low can indicate a reversal and entry against a trade setup. Taking out a prior bar high or low can also be used as a trigger, although I don't find it as powerful as taking out a swing high or low.

Moving Averages

Moving averages can be used in a couple of different ways. Some traders will use a break or close above or below a moving average as an entry trigger. Others will use multiple averages and take a cross of the faster average above or below the slower average(s) as the entry signal.

CCI

There are quite a few traders who use CCI, or the Commodity Channel Index, as taught by Woodie of Woodies CCI Club. There are certain patterns made with this indicator that are considered market entry signals. Some of my traders have been successful in using these signals in coordination with my chat room trade setups. (For more information, you can check out this Web site at www.woodiescciclub.com.)

John Carter and Hubert Senters of www.tradethemarkets.com also have their own unique entry methods that they teach to their students. In spending some time with them in Austin, I got to observe them using their triggers and indicators, which can work very well to trigger entries against price cluster or symmetry setups. As a matter of fact, I thought my trade setups and their triggers complemented each other so well that I decided to merge my chat room with theirs! We now have a rather large chat room that focuses on many different trade entry methods along with

> **Author Tip** There are a number of different entry methods that you can consider using with the trade setups that I have shared with you. What is important is that once you decide on an entry trigger, make sure it is one that you are comfortable with and that you can recognize easily. Make sure it fits your trading personality. After testing its reliability, remain consistent in taking your entries with it.

my Fibonacci trade setups. Some of these trade entries coordinate extremely well with this Fibonacci work. If you want to check out the room, go to www.fibonacciqueen.com.

USING INDICATORS AND TRIGGERS TO FILTER ENTRIES

Let's go over some examples of trade triggers. First let's look at a trade setup. Once a setup is identified, it is time to look for a trigger. Figure 14-1 shows a symmetry trade setup on the three-minute E-mini Russell contract. The projected symmetry resistance comes in at 782.10.

FIGURE 14-1

Let's look at one possible sell trigger for an entry against the 782.10 resistance. This first trigger example is on a two-minute chart of the Russell (see Figure 14-2), where the swing highs and lows might be seen a little more clearly than on the three-minute chart. You can also use a tick or volume chart to find the swing lows or highs to set up your triggers. Personally, I've used anywhere from a 34- to an 89-tick chart when triggering against a Russell or mini-sized Dow setup on a three-minute chart. In other markets, you may need to use a different tick or volume chart.

Note that the high in this setup was made at 782.00, just a tick below the actual symmetry projection. After this high was made (we actually tested the resistance twice in this case), we wanted to look for the market to take out a prior swing low to signal an entry. The swing low I've identified

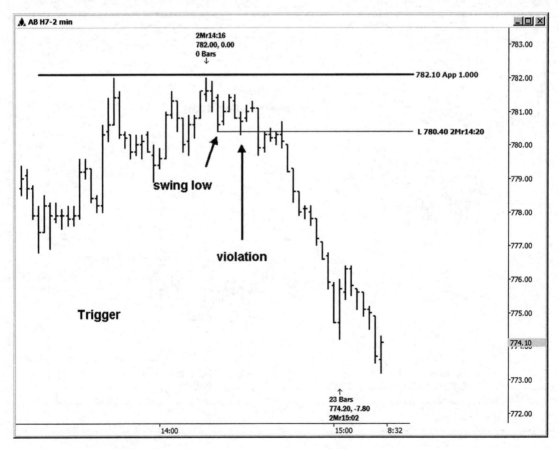

FIGURE 14-2

on this chart is 780.40. When the price fell below this swing low, it signaled a sell entry. Some traders would just place a stop order to enter at 780.30 in this case. The maximum risk would be defined as above the high made prior to the reversal signal. In this case, a stop could be placed just a tick or two above the 782.00 swing high. This risk might be too high for many short-term traders. There are a couple of other options to minimize the risk.

As far as reducing your risk against the original trade setup, there are actually three things you can do.

1. You can simply use a standard price stop. For example, just use a 10- to 15-tick stop on all your trades. If the trade is going to play out, you ideally won't see that much of a pullback before the decline resumes. In this case, a 10-tick stop would have been elected if you went short at 780.30, although a 15-tick stop would still have you in the market.

2. You can use the next lower swing high for a stop that comes in at 781.50 in this example.

3. Rather than selling on the break of the swing low, you can wait for a pullback or retracement after the violation of the prior swing low. The only problem with this third method is that you may never get a pullback, and in that case you will totally miss the trade. Some traders seem to be okay with that and prefer *not* to give up the edge in the market.

When looking at entering on the pullback after the break, I typically look for a retracement of .50 to .786 back from the last swing, and ideally one of those retracements will overlap a 100 percent projection of a prior swing. In this particular example, the pullback terminated right around the coincidence of a .618 retracement back to the original high and a .786 retracement of the prior minor swing that overlapped the 100 percent projection of the move from point a to point b projected from point c (see Figure 14-3). (With an entry closer to the 781.20–781.40 area, you would be risking quite a bit less than if you entered with a stop at 780.30.)

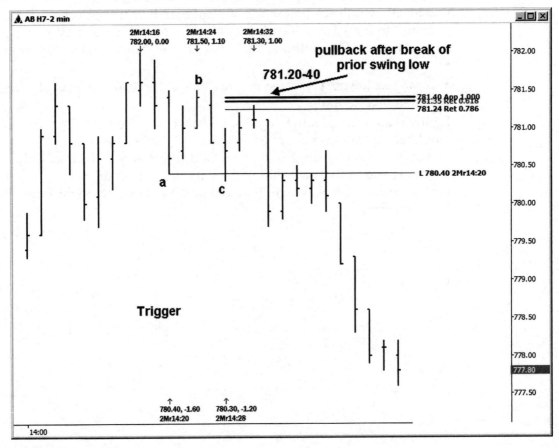

FIGURE 14-3

Let's look at this same setup in Figure 14-4, using a different type of trigger. We are still looking at the same resistance at the 782.10 area, but we would look for a cross of the shorter-term average over the longer-term average to trigger a sell entry. For this example, I used an 8-bar and a 13-bar average. I have labeled the bar where the 8-bar average crossed the 13-bar average. For some, that will be the trigger for a sale against the 782.10 resistance.

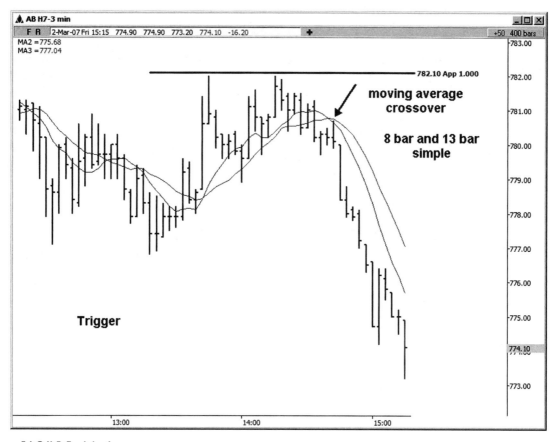

FIGURE 14-4

In Figure 14-5, we are looking at triggering against the same symmetry setup in the E-mini Russell with resistance at 782.10 using one of the TTM entry methods that TTM (tradethemarkets.com) calls the squeeze indicator. Here I used a 500 volume chart with the squeeze indicator. Where I placed the arrows on the chart is where the indicator *fires off* (as they say). This is where you would have entered the sell side on this particular chart.

You can use this indicator on a volume chart, tick chart, or minute chart. To decide which chart or charts to use, you will want to test a variety of them and see which one gives you the type of results you are looking for.

It is sometimes helpful to watch more than one chart for possible entry signals. I also like to use the TTM trend indicator along with the squeeze. I like the visual of the color of the bars changing as the trend is shifting. (Since the chart in this book is gray scale, however, you can't really see the trend indicator on this chart.)

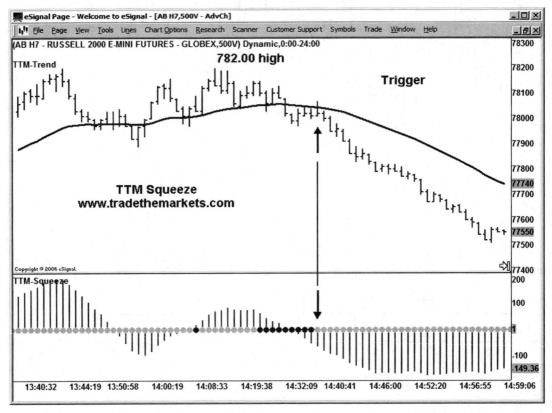

FIGURE 14-5

Let's look at a few more examples of market entries using prior swing lows and highs. Note that once you identify a setup and are in your price decision zone for this setup, you will start looking for a prior swing low or high to trigger your entry. If you are looking at a buy setup, you will be looking for swing highs; if you are looking at a sell setup, you will be looking for swing lows. This swing high or swing low may develop before the trade setup zone is hit or after the zone is met. Either way, it will set up a valid trigger.

Figure 14-6 shows a buy trigger by simply taking out a prior swing high on this one-minute chart of the mini-sized Dow. The first option for an entry would be on a break above the 12145 swing high. You could have

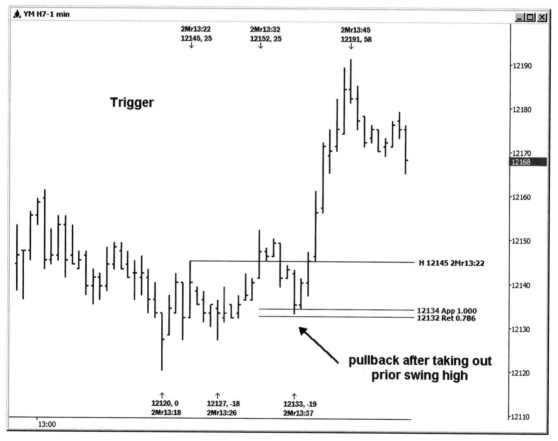

FIGURE 14-6

used a 12146 buy stop for an entry. The initial stop could have been placed below the prior swing low at the 12127 level. This is obviously the riskier entry as it would be around 20 points depending on where you get filled on the stop entry.

The second option for an entry would have been on the first pullback after the 12145 swing high was taken out. In this case, the Dow contract pulled back and held near a coincidence of a .786 retracement back to the prior low along with the 100 percent projection of the prior swing down at the 12132–12134 area. Anywhere from a .50 to a.786 retracement would be a place to look for an entry. The initial stop in this case can be placed just below the 12127 swing low. Let's say you took an entry around the .618 retracement back to the prior low at the 12137 level and your stop is at 12126. The initial risk is then around 11 points, or about half that of the first entry option. Note that stop-loss orders are not always filled at the exact price, so your risk could actually be a bit higher in that case.

In Figure 14-7, an example of using a swing high for an entry trigger is illustrated on a three-minute E-mini Russell contract. Here, trading above the 829.80 swing high would have triggered an entry on the buy side.

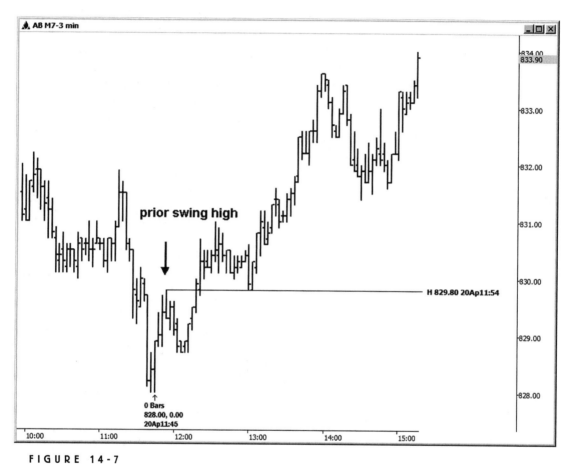

FIGURE 14-7

The alternative entry on the prior E-mini Russell chart would be on a pullback (see Figure 14-8). After the initial breakout above the 829.80 swing high, when you started to see a pullback, you would want to look at entering this pullback anywhere from the 50 percent to the .786 retracement of the prior swing. You can also see if a 100 percent symmetry projection of a prior swing overlaps one of these retracements. (Personally, I gravitate toward whatever retracement overlaps symmetry.) In this case, the 50 percent retracement of the prior low-to-high swing came in at 829.85. This came very close to overlapping the 1.0 projection of the prior swing down at 829.90. You can see the symmetry on the chart, with the first swing down being labeled as 1.10 points and the second swing down labeled as 1.20 points. There is that beautiful symmetry/similarity in the swings. The pullback ended up terminating at 829.80 before the rally resumed.

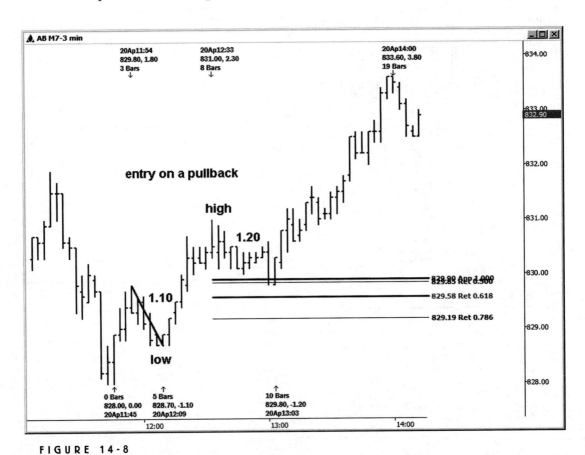

FIGURE 14-8

Figure 14-9 is another example of swing high trigger, illustrated on a three-minute mini-sized Dow contract. The entry would be triggered with a rally above the 12830 swing high in this case.

FIGURE 14-9

If you wanted to wait for the pullback instead, you could have run the retracement of the prior low-to-high swing and also looked for any symmetry projections (see Figure 14-10). In this case, the 100 percent symmetry projection of the prior swing (15 points) was projected from the 12865 high and came in at 12832. This overlapped nicely with the 50 percent retracement of the prior low-to-high swing, which came in at 12831. The pullback terminated right at 12832.

Most of these trigger examples so far have been illustrated on some very short time frame charts. This is because I typically work with day traders all day long, and they don't want to risk a lot of cash on each trade

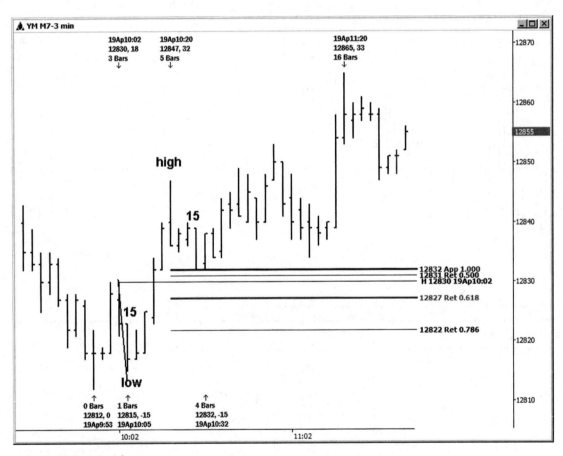

FIGURE 14-10

setup. These same triggers, however, can be used on longer time frame charts. For example, if you have a price cluster setup on a daily chart, you might want to use a 15-minute chart as the trigger for an entry against the daily work. If you are looking at a setup on a 45-minute chart, you might want to use a 5-minute chart for your entry.

Author Tip Remember that you don't want to use these trade triggers by themselves. You always want to start with a trade setup. Using an entry methodology without the Fibonacci work to support it is generally not a high-probability setup.

This next example, Figure 14-11, starts with a price cluster setup on a 15-minute E-mini S&P chart. The price decision zone came in at the 1396.50–1397.00 area. This is also an example that is *not* perfect. The actual high in this case was made 2 ticks below the price cluster zone at 1396.00. As long as you are not a total perfectionist, this is close enough to look for a trade entry trigger.

FIGURE 14-11

In Figure 14-12, we are looking at a 3-minute chart to look for a sell entry against the 15-minute setup in Figure 14-11. We want to use a shorter time frame for a trigger so that we can find an entry that is relatively close to the actual price levels we are basing the trade on. This also typically lowers the risk on the trade entry. There are two swing lows that could have been used for an entry when they were violated. Notice that this time, we did not see a meaningful pullback for an alternative entry. If you didn't just enter on the violation of one of those swing lows, you would have missed out on this trade waiting for a pullback. (Oh, well, there is *always* another trade setup!)

FIGURE 14-12

In the next example, Figure 14-13, we are starting with another price cluster setup on a 15-minute chart in the E-mini S&P contract. Here we had a key support decision at the 1391.00–1391.75 area. In addition, we had a time histogram that was telling us to look for a possible reversal to the upside as we tested this key support. When time and price come together, the odds for a reversal are higher than when you are looking at only time or price parameters by themselves. Let's look at some possible triggers we could have used in this case.

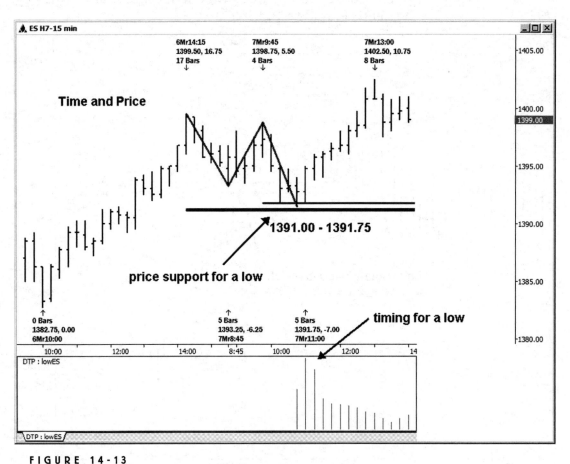

FIGURE 14-13

In Figure 14.14, we are looking at a three-minute chart to watch for a swing trigger entry that might get us into the market relatively close to the price cluster support zone. Here an entry could have been made as soon as the ES traded at 1394.25, which is 1 tick above the prior swing high identified on the chart.

FIGURE 14-14

If you wanted to look at buying the pullback *after* the swing high was taken out, there was an opportunity in Figure 14.15 around the 1394.00 area. This is where a 100 percent projection overlapped a 50 percent retracement of the prior swing. You don't need to be *exact* in your pullback entry. If you tried to wait for an exact move back to the support in this case, you might have missed the entry. (Use common sense in making your decisions.)

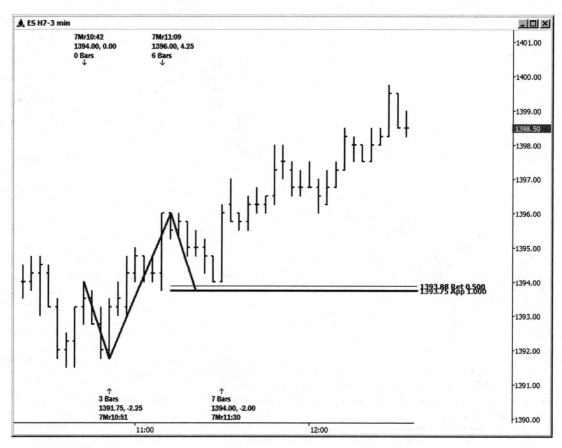

FIGURE 14-15

On this next three-minute chart of the E-mini S&P (see Figure 14-16), I was looking at a symmetry sell setup. Simply taking a couple of the prior corrective rallies on this chart and projecting them from the new low at that time (1425.50 swing low at 12:24 on 3/29/07) gave us our setup on the sell side at the 1429.50–1430.00 area.

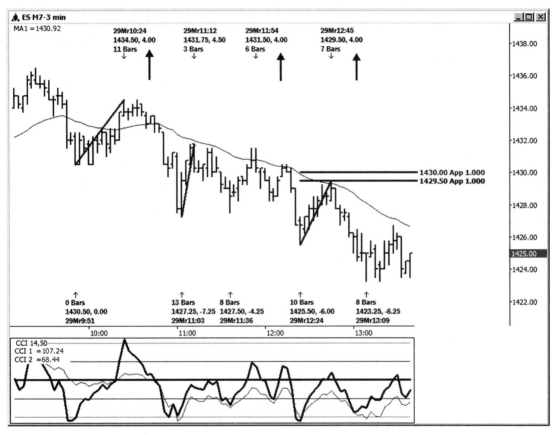

FIGURE 14-16

Now all we need is a trigger that tells us to enter the trade. The first example of a trigger (see Figure 14-17) uses an indicator that is built into the Gold and Platinum Trade Navigator program from www.genesisft.com. (I typically look at color bars when watching this indicator, but since this book will not show the color difference, I have changed the program to illustrate the signal with markers rather than color bars.) The bar that was the sell trigger against the setup was where the marker turned into a triangle pointing downward after a high was made into the trade setup zone at 1429.50. The initial stop on your sell entry would be just a tick above the 1429.50 high. After that, you could either use a trailing stop or use the same type of trigger that got you into the trade setup to exit it. Notice when the triangles switched to back up. This occurred after the 1.272 extension was met on the downside. I marked the exit bar on the chart.

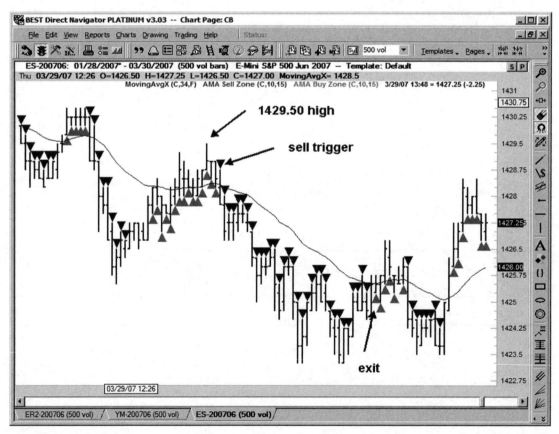

FIGURE 14-17

How about using a swing low trigger on a one-minute chart? From the discussion earlier in this chapter, you know that I like using prior swing lows and highs as entry triggers (see Figure 14-18). Here the entry trigger would have been as soon as we violated the 1428.00 swing low with a print of 1427.75. You could place the initial stop above the 1429.50 swing high, or you might choose to use a price stop. The stop above the prior high would be the safer bet. As far as an exit, I prefer using a trailing stop rather than exiting at a target. The market will often give you a lot more than the first target if it is trending well. The extra cash that you pick up in staying with a winning trade will be a great cushion in your account for those times that the market chops you up a bit.

FIGURE 14-18

One popular CCI sell trigger that has been used by some of my chat room traders is where the 14-bar CCI crosses back below the zero line, joining the 50-bar CCI, which was already below the zero line. You can actually see this trigger on the same chart that the setup developed on (see Figure 14-19). See where the 14-bar (darker indicator) CCI fell back below the zero line; this was your cue to enter the short side. Again, ideally the initial stop would be placed just above the 1429.50 swing high, and a trailing stop can be used to exit.

FIGURE 14-19

Let's take another look at a price cluster setup that developed in Google stock. We actually looked at this example in Chapter 13, but this time we will look at some entry triggers that could have been used (see Figure 14-20). A price cluster developed with the coincidence of three key price relationships between 435.84 and 438.18.

.50 retracement from the 8/3/06 low to the 1/16/07 high = 438.18

1.272 extension from the 12/21/06 low to the 1/16/07 high = 435.84

1.618 extension from the 2/12/07 low to the 2/22/07 high = 436.96

This happened to coordinate beautifully with a time histogram that stood out on 3/5/07 for a possible low to develop. With time and price coming together, what you have to look for next is a trade entry trigger.

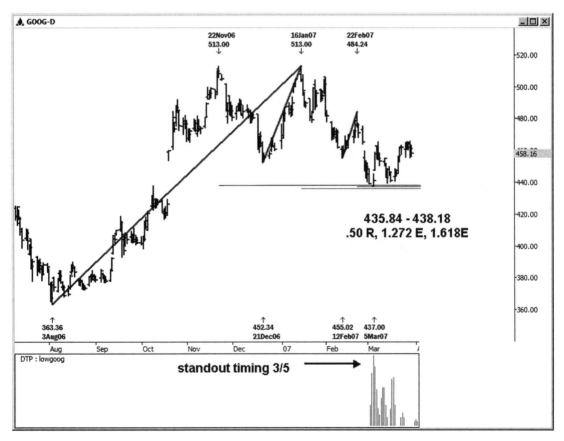

FIGURE 14-20

Again there are a number of different ways that you can trigger into a trade setup. Figure 14-21 is simply a 15-minute chart of GOOG. After making a low on 3/5/07 into both key time and price parameters, the rally above the prior swing high on this chart was the first entry trigger. If you didn't want to buy the breakout above a prior swing, the other option was to buy the pullback after the breakout. The initial stop on either of these entries would be just below the 3/5/07 low made at 437.00. A rally of over $26.00 was seen from this time and price low.

FIGURE 14-21

The next trade setup we are looking at is on the mini-sized Dow contract on a 10-minute chart (see Figure 14-22). After a dramatic rally in this contract, the Dow started to do a bit of a sideways to down move, possibly taking a rest before the trend could resume. Sometimes you don't have a lot of data points to work with on a chart. In this example, by simply running price extensions and 100 percent price projections of points 1 through 5, two price cluster zones developed. One was in the 12492–12494 area with three price relationships, and another developed between 12479 and 12485 with three price relationships. We wanted to watch these zones for a potential low and reversal to the upside to develop from either of these support zones.

FIGURE 14-22

A low was made at 12496, which was 2 ticks above the first price cluster support zone (see Figure 14-23). This was a close enough hit to look for a buy trigger. One simple trigger entry would be when this contract took out the prior swing high at the 12519 level. For example, a trader could put in a 12520 buy stop above that high for an entry. The maximum risk would be defined below the 12496 swing low in this case.

For some day traders, that risk might be a bit high, and you can choose to use a price stop. You might just use an initial stop of 11 to 20 ticks. It all depends on the trader and his or her own comfort level. You probably do *not* want to make it any tighter than 11 ticks, or you are not giving yourself much room for the trade to play out. The initial rally from the 12496 swing low was a 66-tick move, although it eventually saw even higher prices from the original low.

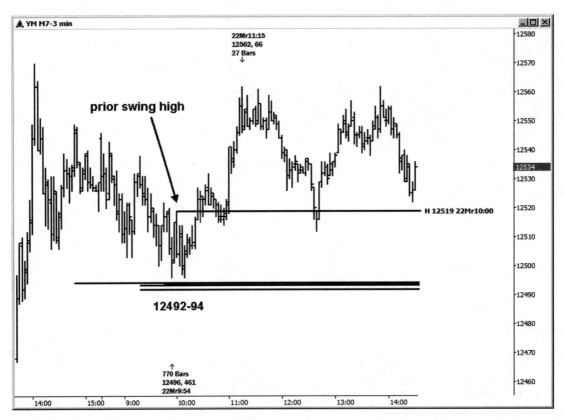

FIGURE 14-23

In this chapter, the trigger examples I've illustrated are only a sampling of what *can* be used for your entries with Fibonacci time and price analysis. For me, they are only part of the trade entry equation. I need to see a few other things before entering against a trade setup. I have a couple of filters that need to be in place at the same time the swing trigger can be taken. My filters are the 34 EMA and the 14- and 50-bar CCI. I watch these filters on a three-minute chart. For a buy, I need to see the price above the 34 EMA when the market triggers and both CCI readings above zero. For a sale, I need to see price below the 34 EMA when the market triggers and both CCI readings below zero.

This is where the ideal trade setup comes in. If you are a day trader and you take only these ideal trade setups in the direction of the next higher time frame, you *should* be able to consistently extract cash from the market. That is, you can do this as long as you are using a good trigger and reasonable stops, and you have good money management skills. This will be discussed further in Chapter 17, which covers using a trading plan. So what is an ideal setup? I need to devote a whole chapter to this high-probability trade setup.

15 CHAPTER

THE IDEAL TRADE SETUP

One of the highest-probability day trading setups that I can share with you, one that I attempt to set up in my chat room every day, is what I call an *ideal setup*. Most days the market provides us with at least a few of these opportunities in each trading session in each market that I am analyzing.

Let's define this setup.

The ideal setup is a basic symmetry setup that occurs on either a three- or a five-minute chart. What makes it an "ideal" setup has to do with the addition of certain indicators. There are essentially four elements that make up this setup that need to be in agreement. They are pattern, symmetry, 34 EMA, and CCI. There are no timing parameters involved in this setup, since I run my time analysis only on my 15-minute charts and higher.

- *First, we look at the three- or five-minute chart and identify the pattern.* If it is making higher highs and higher lows, then we will be looking for a buy setup. If it is making lower lows and lower highs, we will be looking for a sell setup. If the market is going sideways, we will stand aside.

- *Second, we look for the symmetry projections against the trend to identify corrective support or resistance in order to take a position in the direction of the trend.* We are comparing swings in the same direction, and in this case they will be corrective swings within the trend. We are using the 1.0 projection tool looking for similarity or equality in the swings. If we are looking at a bullish pattern of higher highs and higher lows, we will be taking any of the corrective declines within the uptrend and projecting from any new highs to make our symmetry projections for possible buy entries. If we are looking at a bearish pattern of lower lows and lower highs, we will be taking any of the corrective rallies within the downtrend and projecting from any new lows to make our symmetry projections for possible sell entries.

> **Author Tip**   If you run these projections from a new high or low and then the high or low is taken out, you will have to run the projections again and continually update them as the market unfolds. This is one of the reasons traders choose to let me do the work in the chat room, since it becomes tedious, and they would rather focus on trading, not on running the analysis all day long!

- *Third, we want the price of the symmetry projections to be on the right side of the 34 EMA.* If we are setting up the buy side, the price should be above the 34 EMA. If we are setting up the sell side, the price should be below the 34 EMA.
- *Fourth, we want to see the CCI readings on the right side of the zero line.* For this setup, we are watching the 14-bar CCI and the 50-bar CCI. I want to see both the 14- and the 50-bar CCI above the zero line for an ideal buy setup. I want to see both the 14- and the 50-bar CCI below the zero line for an ideal sell setup.

When you see these four elements come together on the short-term charts, you are looking at a relatively high-probability setup. What will raise the odds even higher is if the setup is also in agreement with the pattern on the 15-minute chart. What I mean by agreement is that the price pattern on the 15-minute chart matches what you are seeing on the 3-minute chart. For example, if the 3-minute chart is showing a pattern of higher highs and higher lows, you would also want to see the same pattern of higher highs and lows on a 15-minute chart.

When the two time frames are in agreement in pattern, there will be no argument with the higher time frame trend. This will increase the odds that this setup will play out, and not only for the minimum target, which we usually expect. When this setup is in agreement with the higher time frame trend, this is when we see our trend run days, and the minimum targets for the setup are typically surpassed. The exception to this general rule comes when the 15-minute chart has already met key price extensions of prior swings where moves tend to terminate. In this case, you will be fighting the tendency for the move to terminate on the higher time frame chart since these extensions were met even though the overall pattern may still be bullish. This will not be an issue if you have not yet met the initial targets on the 15-minute chart.

You will see this agreement of time frames occur in some of the following examples. If the 15-minute chart is *not* in agreement with the setup on the 3-minute chart, the higher time frame is working against you, lowering the odds for success. This doesn't mean that the 3-minute setup won't work. It just means that the odds are lower than when you see this agreement of time frames.

With all my trade setups, I recommend using an entry trigger. The trigger can be as simple as taking out a prior swing high or low on a 34-tick chart. Some of my traders use volume charts instead. Some traders use a one-minute chart. We want to use a chart that will show us a trigger relatively quickly and close to the symmetry support or resistance zone so that we are not giving up the "edge" of this trade setup.

I believe that even if you traded only these ideal setups in the direction of the 15-minute chart, you have the raw material to trade successfully and pull out some decent cash from the market. The variables will be the entry trigger you use, the stops, and the money management of the trade.

Typical mistakes I see traders make that could affect their results would be:

1. Using a trigger that gets you into the trade too far away from the support or resistance zone. (This is where you are giving away the edge.)

2. Having stops too tight, so that there is no room for the trade to play out, or having stops too far away, so that you are risking quite a bit more than what you can potentially make on the trade.

3. Taking profits too soon, rather than letting a trade run. Many of these setups can really run for you, with the initial risk being minimal. For example, you can risk 11 to 20 ticks on a trade on the mini-sized Dow and then see a 70-tick rally on a trend day. It would certainly be a shame if you took only 20 ticks profit on the trade when you had the potential to take so much more out of the market. (The extra cash that you can collect from letting a winning trade run can cushion your account against the smaller losses that you will have to take when one of your setups does not work.)

IDEAL TRADE SETUP EXAMPLES

Let's go over some examples of the ideal setup. We will look to make a trade against these setups as long as the symmetry projection is tested and holds. We can't always expect perfect symmetry to unfold in the market, so we do give this trade setup a little leeway. For example, in the E-mini S&P, I would still consider the trade setup valid plus or minus 2 ticks on the zone. In the E-mini Russell and the mini-sized Dow, as long as we are within 2 to 3 ticks of the zone, I will still consider the setup good and look for an entry trigger.

In this first example, Figure 15-1, we are looking at a three-minute chart of the mini-sized Dow. This setup is ideal, as all the elements of the trade have come together. We are looking at a pattern of higher highs and

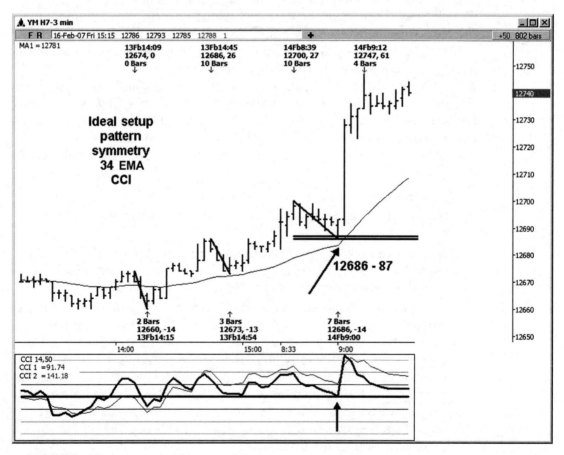

FIGURE 15-1

higher lows. We have symmetry projections that we made from two of the prior declines. These projections, which came in at 12686–12687, are above the 34 EMA at the time we are hitting the support. Also, both the 14- and the 50-bar CCI are above the zero line. In this case, the actual low was made at 12686 and the initial rally off this low was 61 points or ticks.

There is one other thing I would like you to look at in this example. Notice that the symmetry support is very close to the 34 EMA on the test of it. Also note that the 14-bar CCI (the thicker line on the indicator below the chart) has pretty much kissed the zero line and then started moving away from it. This would be called a zero line reject by Woodie's CCI Club (I don't have backtested data on this; however, when you see both the kiss of the 34 EMA and the 14-bar zero line reject within the parameters of an ideal setup in the direction of the 15-minute chart, the odds for the setup playing out seem to be even higher than usual. This is something that I have observed in the five years that I have been running these setups in my chat room.)

Author Tip The bottom line is, don't use this method until you have tested it and proved it to yourself. If you spend some time observing the market and see how many times this setup does occur and play out, you will then have the confidence to take your entry triggers and extract some cash from the market.

Now look real hard at this same Figure 15-1 and you will see that there was another ideal setup. It is where the 12673 low was made. You would have projected the first 14-point decline from the 12686 high. You would have been within a point of the 12673 low, and all the elements of an ideal setup were also present there.

In Figure 15-2, we are looking at another ideal setup on a three-minute chart of the E-mini Russell contract. We are looking at a pattern of lower lows and lower highs in this case. The projection of two prior rallies on this chart set up the possible sell entry area at 816.60. Notice that both of the prior rallies that I used for the projections were 1.90 points. The price of the projections was below the 34 EMA at the time we tested the resistance at the 816.60 area. Both the 14- and the 50-bar CCI readings were below the zero line when we tested the resistance. The result was a high made at 816.60 that was followed by a decline of just over 5.00 points. This chart is also a good example of symmetry. In this case, there were three rally swings that were equal at 1.90 points.

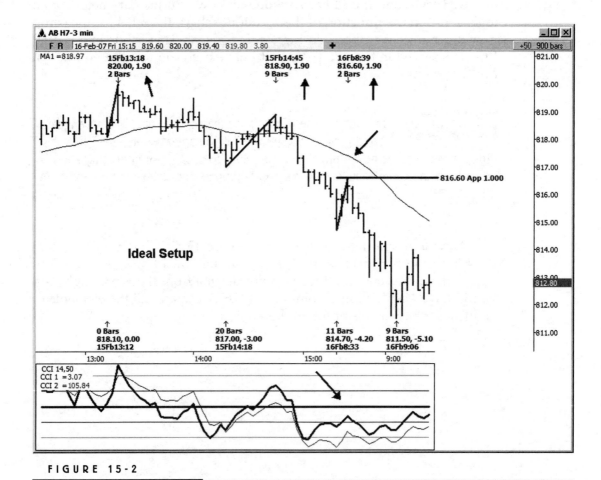

FIGURE 15-2

This next example, Figure 15-3, was a symmetry setup on the three-minute E-mini Russell contract that was not quite ideal. At least, the parameters were not ideal when the zone was initially tested. You can still push the odds in your favor if you follow a couple of rules/guidelines. Notice that the price was slightly above the 34 EMA when it tested the symmetry projection. Also notice that the 14-bar CCI was above the zero line at the time. Those are *not* the ideal parameters for a symmetry trade setup.

You can still look for a sell trigger here as long as when you see the trigger, the price has fallen back below the 34 EMA and the 14-bar CCI has fallen back below the zero line. Notice the decline that eventually followed the high made directly at the symmetry projection at 817.60. It was just over 12.00 full handles, or $1,200.00 per contract. (This is such a simple technique, although it can be extremely powerful if used correctly.)

FIGURE 15-3

Figure 15-4 is another symmetry trade setup that was not ideal at the time the symmetry support was tested. Here, the price was initially slightly below the 34 EMA when we tested the symmetry support, and the 14-bar CCI was initially below the zero line. Notice that when the 14-bar CCI crossed back above zero, the price was also back above the 34 EMA. At *that* time you could elect to take your buy triggers. A rally of 5.00 points was eventually seen after that low was made.

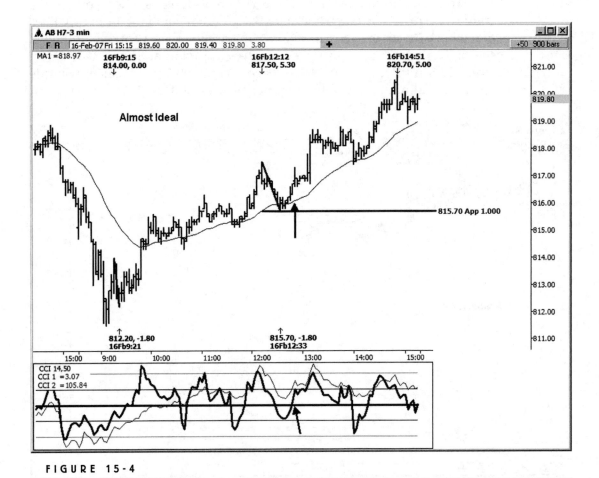

FIGURE 15-4

In Figure 15-5, we are looking at another ideal setup in the E-mini Russell contract. In the chat room, I tend to refer to a setup like this as "micro symmetry." That is because the correction that I have projected from for this setup was relatively small compared to typical corrective swings in this market. In this example, the projection was of a 1.20-point move, or 12 ticks. I projected this prior minor corrective decline from the new high made at 820.00, which gave us a symmetry projection at 818.80. This price was above the 34 EMA, and both CCI readings were above the zero line. The low was made at 818.90—within one tick of the projection. A rally of 8.10 points followed this micro symmetry setup.

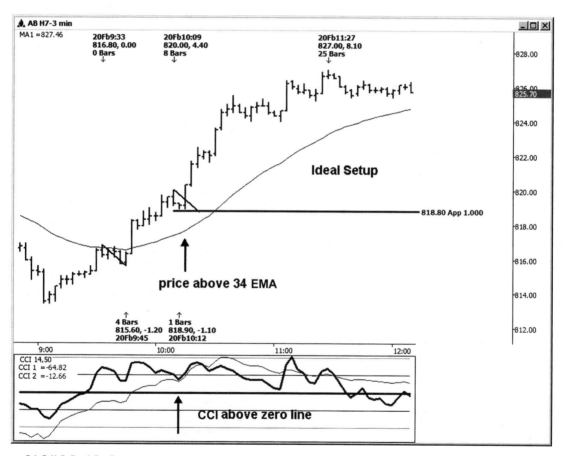

FIGURE 15-5

In Figure 15-6, we are looking at an ideal setup on a three-minute chart of the E-mini S&P contract. In this example, I took two prior corrective declines and projected them from the 1457.00 swing high. This gave us two symmetry support projections at 1455.50 and 1455.75. When the market tested the first support level at 1455.75, the price was above the 34 EMA and the CCI readings were both above zero. Let's say we tested the 1455.50 support instead. This would have been one tick below the 34 EMA. One tick is really not enough to negate this ideal setup. This is where striving for perfection could filter you out of some of the best trade setups. The actual low in this case was made at 1455.75. A rather healthy rally took place after this low was made.

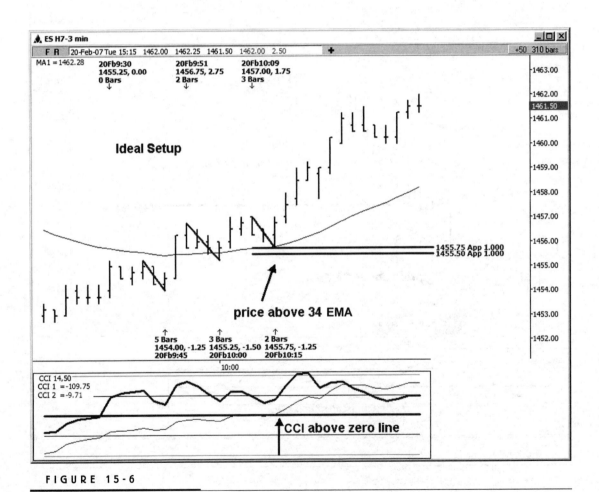

FIGURE 15-6

In Figure 15-7, we are looking at another symmetry setup in the mini contract in crude oil. The symmetry projection for possible support came in at 58.40. When this price support was tested, the 34 EMA was in the right place as we kissed it. The 14-bar CCI, on the other hand, was still below the zero line on the initial test of the support. Notice that when the 14-bar CCI traveled back above the zero line, this contract rallied 93 points from that low made into symmetry.

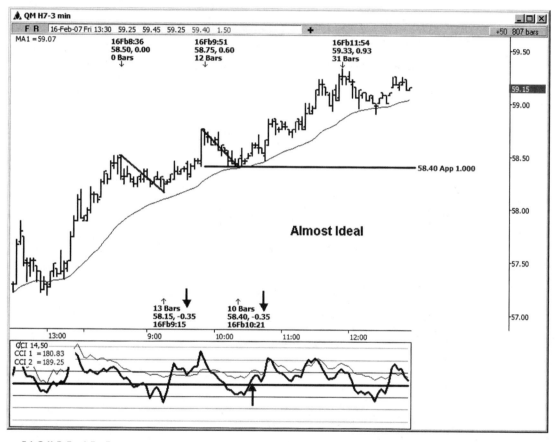

FIGURE 15-7

In Figure 15-8, we are looking at another ideal setup example in the E-mini S&P. Notice that each of the declines labeled on this chart was 1.25 points. When I projected the prior declines from the high made at 1458.75, it projected possible support at the 1457.50 area. When this support was tested, the price was above the 34 EMA and both CCI readings were above zero. (We at least saw the 1.272 target on this setup. When you get used to running the price relationships regularly, you will eventually be able to eyeball where a price relationship should come in!)

Author Tip You can also check the math on that. If you multiplied the 1.25-point decline into the 1457.50 low by 1.272, the result would be 1.59. As long as you rallied for 1.50 from the low, you essentially made the minimum 1.272 target.

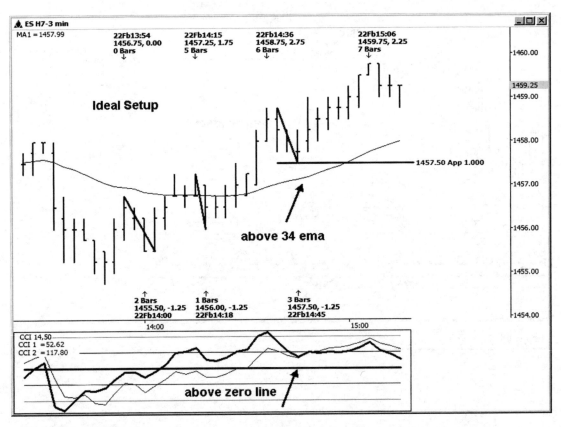

FIGURE 15-8

Figure 15-9 is another example of a symmetry setup in the E-mini S&P contract. Our projections for possible support came in at 1458.75 to 1459.00. When the market tested this support, the price was above the 34 EMA; however, the 14-bar CCI reading was slightly below the zero line. Once the 14-bar CCI crossed back above zero, it was safe to take your entry triggers on your tick chart. (Some traders will actually consider the 14-bar CCI moving back above zero *as* their entry trigger.)

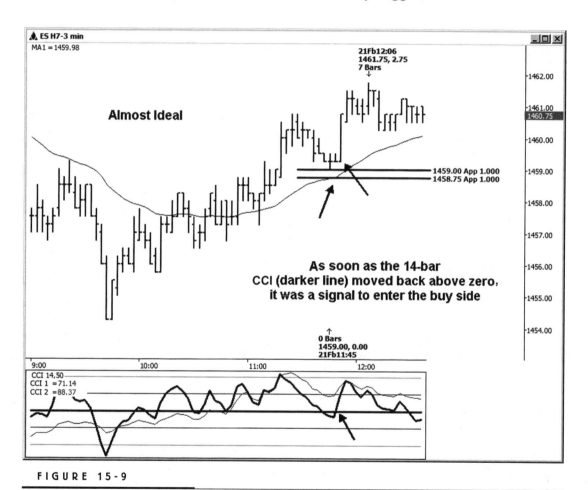

FIGURE 15-9

In Figure 15-10, we are looking at an ideal setup in the mini-sized Dow contract. Take a look at the prior declines that are labeled in this chart. They were 12, 10, and 9 points. These declines were then projected from the 12704 swing high. When this support at the 12692–12695 area was tested and held, the price was above the 34 EMA, and both the CCI readings were above zero. An 18-point rally followed a low that was made at 12695.

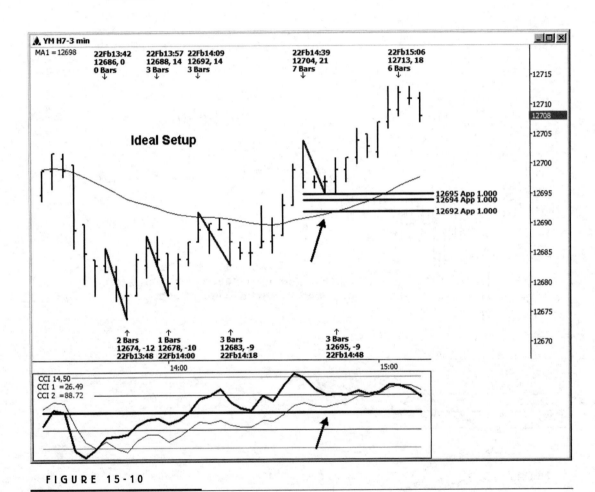

FIGURE 15-10

Figure 15-11 was another ideal setup in the mini-sized Dow. There were a few symmetry projections that could be made from the 12779 swing high for possible support. I have the important one labeled—that is the one that the price held above. Notice that both the 34 EMA and the CCI were in the right place when the support was tested. A 20-point rally was seen from the 12765 low, which was made just 1 tick above the key symmetry support projection.

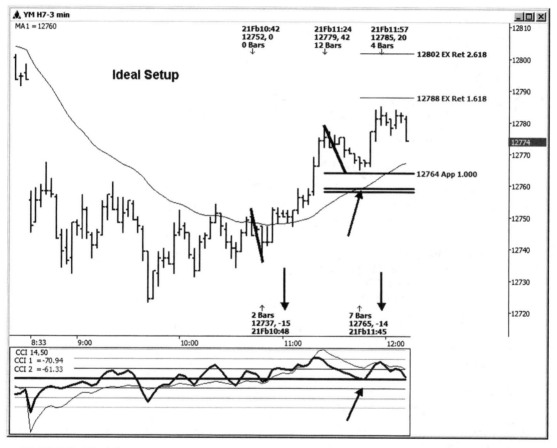

FIGURE 15-11

Let's look at how the agreement of the 15-minute chart can help get you into some great trend run moves. In Figure 15-12, we are looking at a 15-minute chart of the mini-sized Dow. On 2/22/07, the pattern on the 15-minute chart shifted from higher highs and higher lows to lower lows and lower highs when the 2/21/07 swing low was violated. With that shift in pattern favoring the bears, we wanted to focus on the ideal sell setups on the three-minute charts.

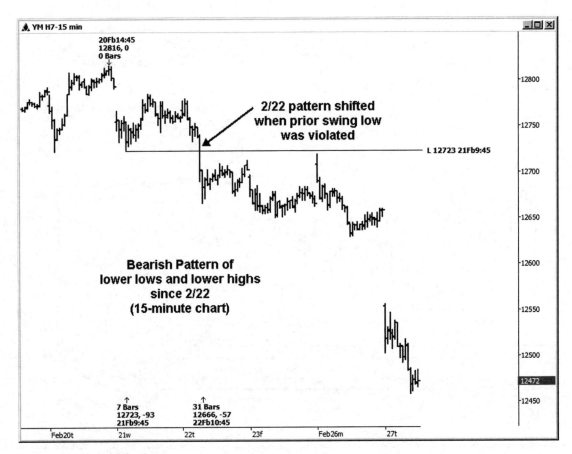

FIGURE 15-12

Figure 15-13 shows the three-minute mini-sized Dow chart. On 2/27/07, we were looking at an ideal setup that was in *agreement* with the bearish pattern we looked at in Figure 15-12. The price projections of the prior corrective rallies showed us possible resistance at the 12484–12489 area. When the market tested this key resistance, the price was below the 34 EMA and the CCI readings were also below zero. From this one setup, a 383-point decline was eventually seen from a high made at 12485.

I'm sure it was difficult for most traders to hold on to the position long enough for the full ride, although the opportunity existed. This decline was obviously way more than the initial downside target for the trade setup. The initial target would have been 1.272 of the swing into the high, which was 27 points. If you multiply 27 × 1.272, 34 and change comes up as the initial target. If you exited that trade at the initial target, you left quite a bit of cash on the table. This is the reason why you want to trade multiple contracts and leave a portion on to let the trade run for you.

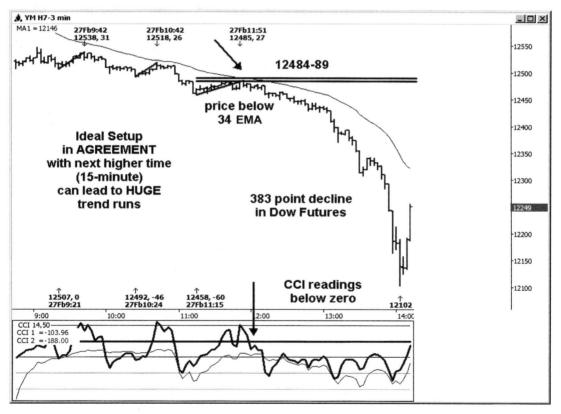

FIGURE 15-13

Figure 15-14 is an example of an ideal setup on a three-minute chart in the mini-sized Dow. When the key price support at 12298 was tested, the price was above the 34 EMA and both CCI readings were above zero. After an initial rally (40 points) off this support, however, the trade failed to reach the initial upside target. This is why we need to be aware of what the longer time frame charts look like. (They were not truly in agreement with this bullish trade setup.)

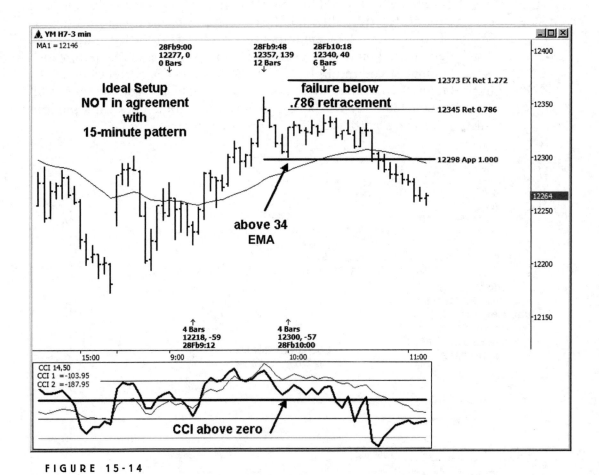

FIGURE 15-14

The ideal setup on the YM in Figure 15-14 did not truly have the agreement of the 15-minute chart to support the trade setup. First, you can see that on the 15-minute chart, the price was below the 34 EMA and the 50-bar CCI was below zero. The general pattern of this chart was lower lows and lower highs. The place where you could try to justify the buy side would be where you have a minor pattern of higher highs and higher lows from the 2/27 low. But let's take a look at another Dow chart (Figure 15-15) and use some common sense.

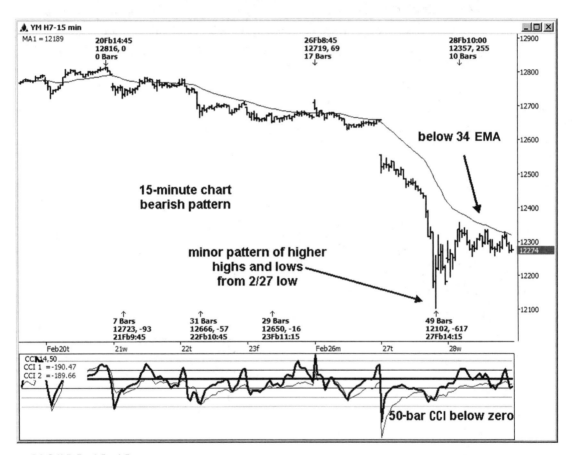

FIGURE 15-15

Figure 15-16 shows you what kind of market we were looking at in the bigger picture. Looking at this daily chart in YM, you can see that this market had been severely damaged after the 2/20/07 high was made. This damage became obvious on 2/27/07 when the prior swing low was violated on the daily chart at 12561. The ideal setup example in the previous two charts that failed occurred after 2/27/07.

Author Tip   Do you really think you would want to be focusing on buy setups after this type of damage had been sustained? I know that for some people, the answer would be yes. Countertrend trades can work for those who are nimble, but why trade when the odds are not clearly on your side?

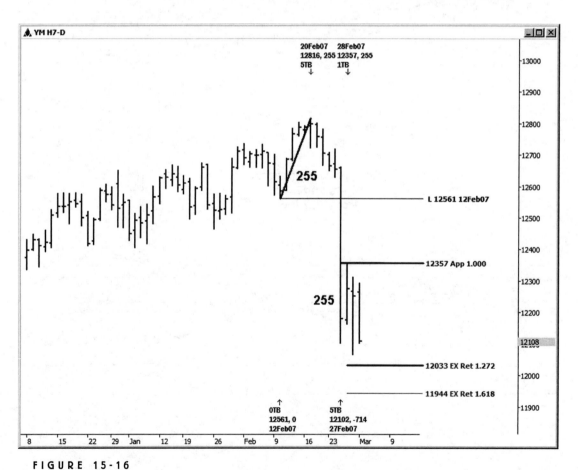

FIGURE 15-16

These next ideal trade setups also occurred after 2/27/07 (see Figure 15-17). This mini-sized Dow setup definitely looked ideal. You had the short-term pattern in your favor, the price was above the 34 EMA, and the CCI readings were above zero. It looked like a great setup on the three-minute chart.

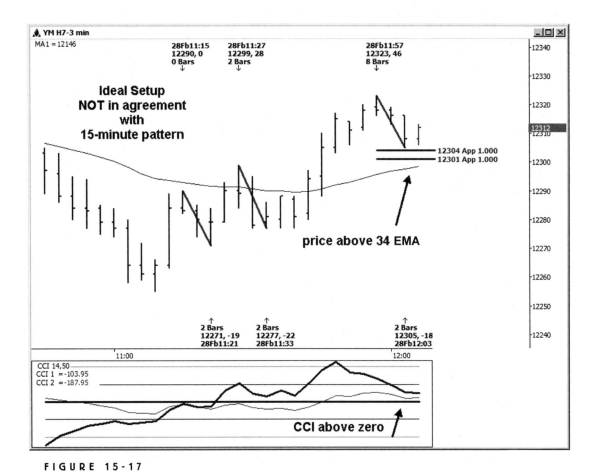

FIGURE 15-17

This setup was too good to be true, however, as the longer time frame charts essentially were *not* in agreement with a buy setup. The key support was violated, and the setup did not play out (see Figure 15-18).

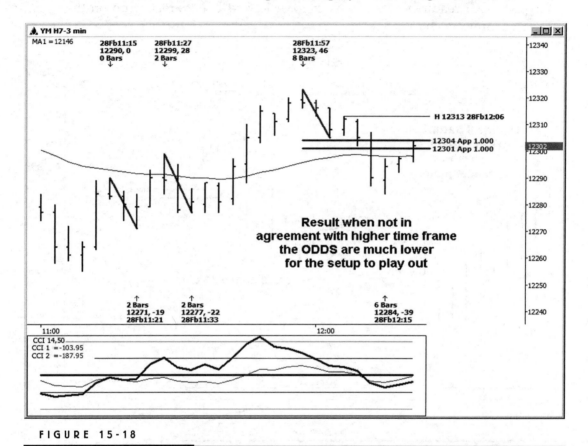

FIGURE 15-18

This chapter defined what I call an ideal setup. It is a variation of a symmetry trade setup specifically for day traders. These parameters are valid only for a three- or five-minute chart. If you are a very conservative day trader/scalper, it will be worth waiting for these ideal setups to show up in the market, since the agreement of the parameters in the "ideal setup" makes this a relatively high-probability setup. Don't forget to wait for your trigger entries before stepping up to the plate!

16 CHAPTER

FROM ANALYSIS TO TRADE ENTRY—PUTTING IT ALL TOGETHER

What I would like to do in this chapter is give you an idea of the thought process that you can go through from start to finish, from creating a trade setup to entry. Here I will attempt to walk you through my thought process. First, let's review the steps you will need to take to find or identify your trade setups.

STEPS FOR IDENTIFYING YOUR TRADE SETUPS

1. Identify key highs and lows on the chart you are analyzing.
2. Run all possible Fibonacci price relationships.
3. Look to identify trade setups.
4. Run Fibonacci time relationships for added confirmation (optional).
5. If a setup is identified, look for an entry trigger.

   Let's break down these steps individually.

1. *Identify the key highs and lows from which to run price and time relationships.*
2. *Run all the Fibonacci price relationships for possible support and resistance levels, using the key highs and lows that you identified in step 1.*

   To set up support for possible buy setups:

   Run all possible price retracements from the low to high swings (.382, .50, .618, .786).

Run all possible price extensions from the low to high swings (1.272, 1.618).

Run all possible price projections from the high to low swings, projected from another high (1.0, 1.618).

To set up resistance for possible sell setups:

Run all possible price retracements from the high to low swings (.382, .50, .618, .786).

Run all possible price extensions from the high to low swings (1.272, 1.618).

Run all possible price projections from the low to high swings, projected from another low (1.0, 1.618).

> **Author Tip** Ideally, you want to set up your trade entries in the direction of the trend. You can also run the Fibonacci price relationships that are counter to the trend for help in exiting your trades. I realize that there are some traders who will want to use the Fibonacci time and price work to set up countertrend trades. Just keep in mind that the odds for success with setups that are counter to the trend will be lower than with the setups in the direction of the trend. If you are a new trader, leave countertrend trading to the professionals.

If a market is moving sideways, you can still run the price relationships on both sides and see if a trade setup becomes obvious, although the odds will not be as high as if you are working with a clearly trending market. In a sideways market, there is generally a healthy battle going on between the bulls and the bears. It is a bit easier to get chopped up in this type of environment. It is better to wait for a clear decision out of the sideways move before getting involved.

3. *Once you have run all the possible price relationships, look for one of these trade setups:*

Price cluster setup

Symmetry setup

Two-step pattern setup

You can stop here if you like. Fibonacci price setups by themselves work just fine when you coordinate them with your tested entry triggers. If you want just a bit more of an edge, however, invest some time in running the analysis on the time axis of the market.

4. *Run the Fibonacci time relationships.*

You will most likely be running the time cycles from the same key highs and lows that you identified for your price work. Use a bit of common sense in running the timing work, keeping in mind the nuances discussed in the chapters on timing.

Time cycles from two points (0.382, 0.50, 0.618, 0.786, 1.0, 1.272, 1.618):

High to high

Low to low

High to low

Low to high

Time cycles from three points (1.0, 1.272, 1.618):

Low to high from another low, comparing swings in the same direction (alternate time projections)

High to low from another high, comparing swings in the same direction (alternate time projections)

High to high from an intervening low

Low to low from an intervening high

Look for a cluster of time-cycle relationships and see if it supports any of your price work. A trade setup is still valid even if it is not supported by timing. If the timing coincides with it, however, the odds for a reversal are higher. If you have the Dynamic Trader software, you can run a timing histogram instead of running the time-cycle work.

For myself, to do a complete analysis of a market, I like to do a weekly chart, a daily chart, and a few intraday charts. In the stock index futures, those will typically be a 135- or 45-minute chart, a 15-minute chart, and a 3-minute chart. The weekly chart will give me a good view of the bigger picture. The daily chart will also give me a good idea of the slightly larger trend, and this is where I will run my main timing work. The intraday charts will help me set up trade entries that are relatively low risk and that ideally are in agreement with the longer time frame work.

INTRADAY CHART EXAMPLES

I have chosen those particular intraday charts for the stock indexes so that my intraday timing work will be more accurate, as the time frames divide equally into the trading session, as discussed in Chapter 12. For other markets, you may want to use different time frames on the intraday charts. For example, in FOREX, you might use a 120-minute chart and a 60-minute chart. My main markets have always been the stock indexes, so I have been less concerned with the time period charts for other markets where I am not running any intraday timing work. Use a little common sense here and choose a chart where you can clearly see the swings you want to work with.

Looking at this 15-minute chart in the E-mini S&P (see Figure 16-1), the first thing that catches my eye is the pattern. We are looking at a bullish pattern of higher highs and higher lows from the 1506.50 low. Since I prefer to set up my trade entries in the direction of the main trend, the first thing I want to do is set up the buy side of the market by running all possible price retracements, extensions, and projections for possible support and entries on the buy side. This way I can look to enter in the direction of the main trend on a pullback.

FIGURE 16-1

Let's start with the obvious retracements. First I'll run the retracements of the move from the 1506.50 low to the 1542.00 high, which are illustrated in Figure 16-2. I was looking for possible support.

FIGURE 16-2

In Figure 16-3, I ran the retracements of another swing from low to high (from the 1512.50 low to the 1542.00 high), looking for overlapping price relationships and possible support. These price relationships did not end up in the price cluster that I will be illustrating, although this was still an important analysis step.

FIGURE 16-3

Next, I wanted to run any price extensions of prior low-to-high swings for possible support (see Figure 16-4). Here I ran the extensions off the move from the 1535.75 low to the 1538.75 high. Note that the 1.272 is not showing, since the price had already violated that level at the time of the analysis. Once a level has been violated by a decent margin, I simply erase it.

FIGURE 16-4

On this next chart (Figure 16-5), it might be a bit difficult to see, but I saw an opportunity to run another price extension of the move from the 1536.50 low to the 1542.00 high for possible support. In this case also, you will not see the 1.272 extension, since the price had already traded below that level.

FIGURE 16-5

I've already run my retracements and price extensions. It's time to look for any projections that would make sense. In Figure 16-6, I show you where I ran a 1.0 projection of a prior corrective decline, looking for possible support. Here I ran the 1.0 projection of the swing from the 1521.00 high to the 1512.50 low (an $8.50-point swing), projected from the 1542.00 high. I used only the 1.0 projection in this case because I typically run only the symmetry projections when I am attempting to enter the main trend on a pullback. I use the 1.618 projection more in looking for the termination of a move.

FIGURE 16-6

Since I also started to see a bit of a zigzag pattern and a possible two-step, I ran another minor 1.0 projection of the swing from the 1542.00 high to the 1535.75 low, projected from the 1538.75 high, for possible support (see Figure 16-7).

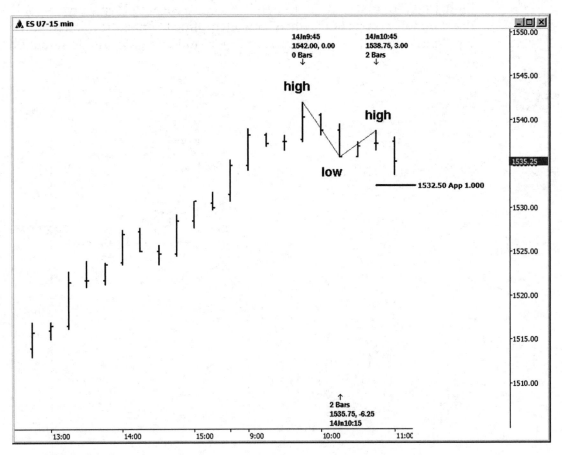

FIGURE 16-7

The end result of all the price work was a two-step pattern cluster, along with some healthy confirming relationships from some of the other meaningful swings. The price support zone came in at 1532.50–1533.90, which is illustrated on the 15-minute chart in Figure 16-8. In my chat room, I generally round out the numbers to the nearest tick. Since the S&P ticks are in quarters, I would call it 1532.50–1534.00. The price relationships were:

.236 retracement of the 1506.50 low to the 1542.00 high = 1533.62
1.618 extension of the 1535.75 low to the 1538.75 high = 1533.90
1.618 extension of the 1536.50 low to the 1542.00 high = 1533.10
1.0 projection of the 1521.00 high to the 1512.50 low, projected from the 1542.00 high = 1533.50
1.0 projection of the swing from the 1542.00 high to the 1535.75 low, projected from the 1538.75 high = 1532.50

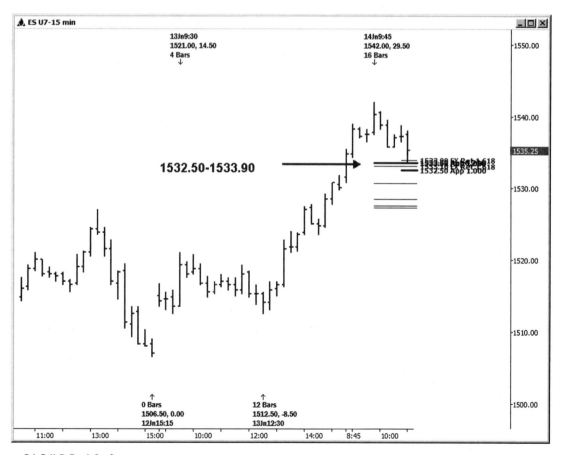

FIGURE 16-8

In Figure 16-9, I used the Dynamic Time Projection tool on my program and ran the Fibonacci time cycles from the most recent high at the 1542.00 level. There were two standout time zones for a possible low that you can see by looking at the histogram below the price area of this chart. The first standout on the histogram coordinated beautifully with a test of the key price support zone. The actual low was made at 1533.75, within one 15-minute bar of the standout histogram bar.

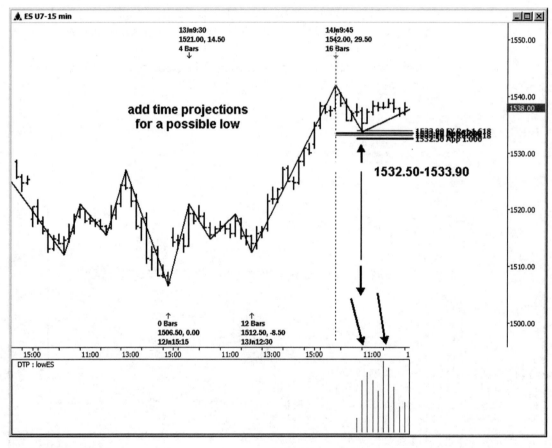

FIGURE 16-9

280

Figure 16-10 shows the initial rally that we saw from this intraday time and price setup. The first rally lasted 5.75 points.

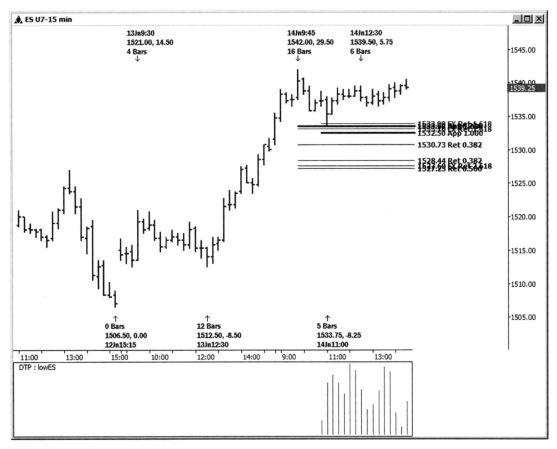

FIGURE 16-10

After a slight pullback to the cluster low, the ES eventually rallied 20.25 points from this time and price setup (see Figure 16-11).

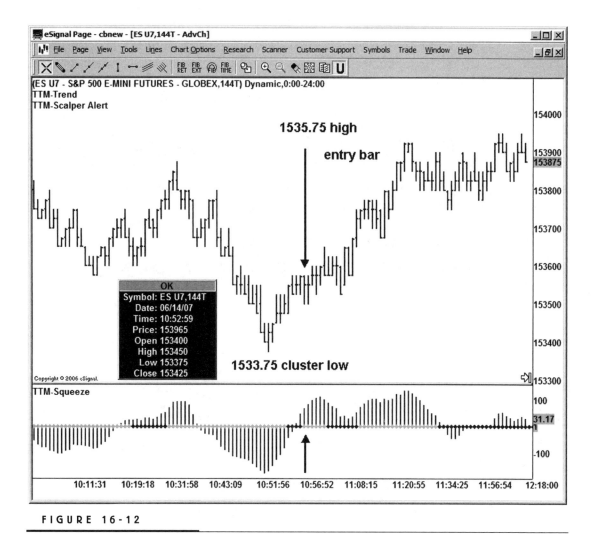

FIGURE 16-12

We knew that we had the time and price support to consider a buy entry in this market. What I needed to see in order to enter a trade according to *my* trading plan was a price trigger. Figure 16-12 is an example of a price trigger I like to use that I learned from John Carter and Hubert Senters. It is called a squeeze trigger. When I'm looking for an entry into a trade setup on a 15-minute chart, I like to use either a 144- or a 233-tick chart in the E-mini S&P. The arrow on the bottom of this chart indicates where the squeeze trigger "fired off."

In this case, the worst fill if you entered on that bar would be at the high of the bar, which was 1535.75. This entry was two full points away from the price cluster low. Since I knew that the initial upside target was at least 10 points from the low made at 1533.75, I considered this close enough to the price cluster support to take the entry.

Now that we've walked through an example of creating and entering a trade setup from start to finish, the next question would be, how do you manage a trade once you are in it? The next chapter will include suggestions on managing a trade once you are in it and will also stress the importance of having a written trading plan.

17 CHAPTER

BEATING THE ODDS WITH A TRADING PLAN

I am told by many broker friends that a high percentage of their clients lose money in the market. Some estimate that 85 to 95 percent of their clients will lose their stake in trading within a year. I don't know where to find the statistics that validate this opinion, but I've certainly heard similar percentages and estimates over the years.

Let's make the assumption that this information is not far from the truth. If the odds are so highly stacked against a new trader, what do you need to do to put the odds back in your favor and increase your chances of success in this business?

This question brings me to one of my new favorite card games, which is Texas Hold 'Em. Texas Hold 'Em is a poker game in which understanding and acting on the proper odds can bring the player success. Many professional players make a solid living playing this game, which was made famous by the World Series of Poker broadcasts. One of the first lessons I learned when I started my education in poker was the importance of your starting hand. The starting hand is the two cards that are dealt to everyone on the poker table before the first round of betting begins. If you have a good starting hand in poker, then you have a reason to bet in the game, since the odds are in your favor. If you don't have a good starting hand, then you should fold, or throw those cards away.

To relate Texas Hold 'Em to trading, if you have a good trade setup, it's like having a good starting hand in poker. You then have a reason to consider placing a bet in the market. If you don't have a good trade setup, you should stand aside and wait until you do. Occasionally in my chat room, I will remind my traders that entering a trade without waiting for a setup is like playing a round of poker without a good starting hand: the odds are certainly not in your favor!

DESIGN YOUR TRADING PLAN

If you are going to take trading seriously, the first thing you need is a trading plan that puts the odds for success in your favor.

There are three main elements that should be part of your trading plan. The plan should define (1) your trade setup or setups, (2) your trade triggers and filters, and (3) your money management rules and techniques.

Trade Setup

Your trade setup is your recognition of a potential opportunity in the market. If you are using my methodology, a setup would be a price cluster setup, a symmetry setup, or a two-step pattern setup. Your setup needs to be defined in your plan.

Trade Triggers

Your trade trigger is what tells you to take action (entry) on a particular setup. Chapter 14 covered the many different types of trade triggers that you can use in your trading plan. You need to choose a method of trade entry that you are comfortable with and that you can easily recognize. Also, if you have any technical filters that you use to define whether or not you are allowed to take an entry according to your plan, include them here. A filter might be something as simple as whether or not you are above or below the 34 EMA.

Money Management

The money management segment of your plan should include the following:

- *Position size.* Make sure your unit size is appropriate for the size of the account you are trading. (A good broker might be able to offer you some sound advice on this matter. Better yet, find a book on the subject if you don't have a good handle on what this means.)
- *Initial stop-loss orders.* You need to define your risk on each trade. Your initial stop-loss order should be placed immediately after you enter a trade, or simultaneously if possible, through your electronic trading platform or front-end software technology.

> **Author Tip** There are some traders who believe in either using "mental stops" or not using stops at all. This may work for a very few lucky individuals, but I do *not* recommend it. For most traders, this is a disaster waiting to happen.

- *Trailing stops.* Trailing stops can be used to protect your profits and/or as a trade exit strategy. If you are going to use a trailing stop, you need to define when you are going to move the initial stop and either by how much or to where you will move it and why. It is common for a trader to trail up to a breakeven stop once a market starts to go in his or her favor, which typically means at least a few ticks, pips, or cents of profit from the original entry price. (Your trading platform or front-end software package can do most of this for you automatically once you define the parameters within the program.)
- *Trade targets and exit strategies.* You should always have an idea of what you can expect from a trade. You may not always get your target, but it does give you an idea as to whether your risk/reward ratio on the trade is adequate. Typically traders will tell you that they expect to make three or four times the amount that they are risking with their initial stop. That should pretty much be the minimum you should shoot for. If you are risking too much for too little, you are likely to donate all of your trading capital to the market eventually. So at least start with a first target to help you define your risk/reward ratio. Many traders will have more than one target. In my work, I have three (1.272, 1.618, and 2.618).

> **Author Tip** Some traders will simply choose to exit a trade when their target is met. Other traders will simply tighten up a trailing stop when a target is neared and allow the market to decide whether or not to give them more of a profit. If you are trading more than one unit, you can get a bit fancier with money management. Some traders will exit part of their position at either a designated monetary target or the first trade target. Then they might use a trailing stop on the balance of the position and see how much the market gives them on the rest of the trade. Be sure your exit strategy fits your trading personality.

TWEAKING YOUR PLAN

Once you have your trading plan in writing, it may need to be tweaked just a bit. Since there are so many different variables in the plan, by the time you include all the money management decisions, these variables sometimes need to be adjusted to achieve better results. For example, you may find that a trade entry trigger on a tick or volume chart may get you into a trade setup sooner than a trigger on a minute chart, so you would alter your plan to reflect that. Another example would be to change the parameters for your initial stop-loss orders. There are times when traders will use such a tight stop that they are inviting the market to stop them out more often than not. Adjusting to a more reasonable stop in this case can increase the trader's odds for success.

The bottom line is this: if you are not getting the results you desire with your current plan, take a look at where you are having problems, then focus on that and see what adjustments you can make.

Some questions you can ask yourself are:

- Am I getting stopped out too often?
- Am I exiting the trades too early?
- Are my trailing stops too tight?
- Are my trade entries late?
- Are my losses too large compared to my winners?

Last but not least, test-drive your plan before you put any *real* cash on the line, and test it again after making any changes. Your broker can set you up with a trading simulator for this purpose, or you can always log the results by hand if there is no easier way to keep track of your testing results.

DISCIPLINE

A trader needs the discipline to follow the trading plan; otherwise the plan is worthless. First, there is the discipline to recognize and act on your trade setups when they are triggered, and then there is the discipline to follow up with your money management rules. If you choose to use a front-end software program to assist you in trading, most or all of the money management part of the plan can be automated with that program.

Personally, when I find time for any intraday trades, I like to use Ninja Trader with the advanced trade management features to handle all my decisions beyond the initial trade entry. The initial trade entry is *not* automated for me, since I need to identify a trade setup and then a trigger that tells me to enter the trade. Every other decision after that *can* be automated. Let's look at what a good front-end trading software program can do for you.

NINJA TRADER SOFTWARE

The Ninja Trader software (www.ninjatrader.com) is much more than a basic trade entry platform and has many powerful features, but my focus in this book is on its trade management capabilities. Trade management is what takes place once a trade has been initiated; it dictates the parameters and process for exiting the trade. I consider this aspect of the program to be *extremely* valuable, as it is essentially building in your discipline for you because once you make the initial trade entry, the software will now manage the trade to its conclusion, thus removing emotion and the potential for human error.

It does so through its Advanced Trade Management (ATM) feature, which allows you to predefine the trade management parameters of your own trades in ATM templates. Specifically, within the ATM template, the trader will predefine the financial risk/reward ratio with a stop-loss order (risk) that will be placed immediately once the initial entry is made and a profit target order (reward) that is entered simultaneously. These two orders will bracket and protect the open position. In addition, the template also allows the trader to predefine very specific parameters for exiting the trade.

You can create very advanced stop-loss strategies with either single-step or multistep increments, creating a "trailing stop." A trailing stop will automatically adjust your stop-loss order higher as the trade becomes profitable to limit your downside risk and maximize your profit potential. Ninja Trader ATM is intelligent, will keep track of all orders, and will automatically adjust them in price or position size as the trade progresses. It is critical that traders take control of their emotions and are disciplined if they want to be successful. The Ninja Trader application is designed for this purpose and is an important tool that you can add to your trading toolbox to help you significantly in these areas. Because it plays such a powerful role in alleviating emotional and discipline issues, it could actually mean the difference between being a profitable trader and an unprofitable trader.

An example of a Ninja Trader ATM strategy can be seen in the bottom portion of Figure 17-1 in the ATM Strategy Parameters section of the SuperDOM (the SuperDOM is the entire entry screen). This ATM entry strategy is very straightforward, and in this case was entered for an E-mini S&P trade. It states that there will be two profit targets and that upon entry to the market, they will be placed 4 and 8 ticks above the average entry price. It also states that there will be two stop-loss orders, and in this case both will be placed 4 ticks below the average entry price. Once the trade is

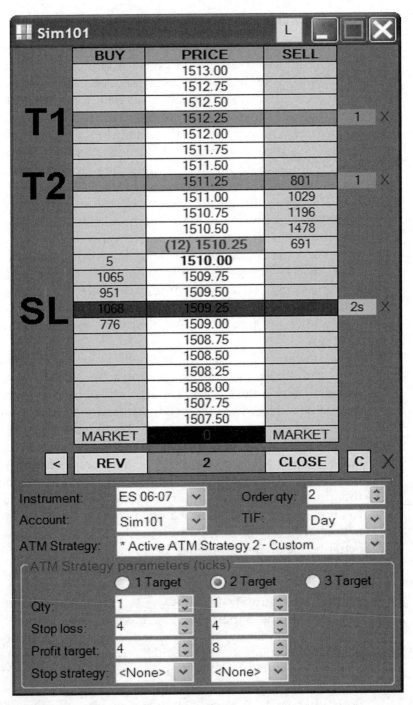

FIGURE 17-1

executed and filled, these orders, which have been predefined in the ATM template, are immediately placed as shown. The average entry price is 1510.25, and the profit target and stop loss orders have been correctly entered as specified in the ATM template. You will notice that the Stop Strategy boxes are set to none, but this is where auto-breakevens, trailing stops, and other advanced exit parameters can also be predefined.

In Figure 17-2, the same ATM entry strategy has been used, but in this case it was executed through Ninja Trader's chart-based order entry screen. Chart-based trading is gaining in popularity, and Ninja Trader has augmented its powerful charting functionality with this highly desirable option.

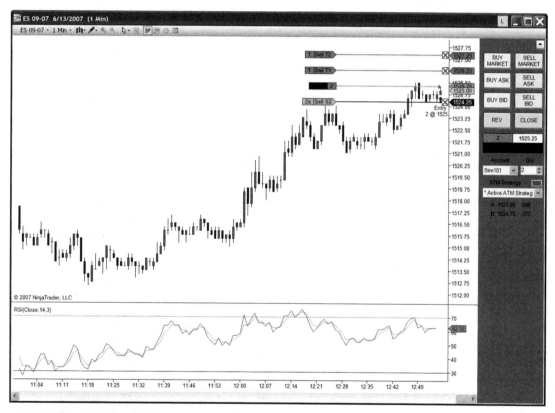

FIGURE 17-2

TRADING PSYCHOLOGY

When I talk about trading psychology, I am talking about your internal belief systems, the patterns or programs that you carry inside yourself that can affect your trading results either positively or negatively.

Many successful traders in this industry have addressed the issues of their psychology or internal beliefs. This is a place that most traders eventually come to after either struggling with losses or being unable to break through to the higher level of success that they want to achieve. I believe that this is the *most* important ingredient for success in this business. Mark Douglas has written extensively on the subject of trading psychology. I would recommend reading both *The Disciplined Trader* and *Trading in the Zone* for some insight on this topic.

There are a few other methods and techniques that could assist a trader as far as the psychological issues of trading are concerned. Doing a search on the Internet with the keywords "trading psychology" could help you in that area. Personally, I highly recommend looking into what Carol (Libby) Adams does with her NLP work at ww.academyofselfknowlege.com.

In conclusion, I have provided you with a formula for stacking the odds in your favor:

1. A solid trading *methodology*: Fibonacci time and price analysis. This methodology not only clearly defines your risk in the market, but also provides targets and goals for your trading plan. This methodology has been covered in detail in Chapters 1 to 16.

2. Keys to writing up your *trading plan* with all the variables clearly defined. With a written trading plan, there should be no question about what trade setups you should be considering, or when to enter or exit a trade, or even how and when to use a trailing stop.

3. An understanding of the importance of having a *positive trading psychology* to support your success. I am told by many well-respected traders that psychology is at least 85 percent of the game. Addressing psychological issues is a very important and personal journey for each individual trader.

4. An understanding of the importance of *discipline*—having the discipline to follow your written plan for success. A great methodology and solid trading plan are worth something only with the discipline to execute the plan as it is written.

These four elements of the formula are a recipe for success and for putting the odds in your favor in trading the markets. My hope is that you will apply some or *all* of the techniques I have shared with you and profit greatly from their use. I hope to meet some of you soon, either at a trading conference or at a Texas Hold 'Em table in Las Vegas!

I wish you great luck and success in your own personal journey into trading the markets.

INDEX

ABOUT THE AUTHOR

Carolyn Boroden is a commodity trading advisor and technical analyst specializing in Fibonacci time and price analysis. Her focus is on the "synchronicity" or confluences of both price and time relationships that identify relatively low-risk, high-probability trading setups. Ms. Boroden has been involved in the trading industry since 1978. Her background includes working on the major trading floors, including the Chicago Mercantile Exchange, the Chicago Board of Trade, NYFE, and COMEX.

For four years, Ms. Boroden taught a segment of the Chicago Commodity Boot Camp seminars on advanced trading techniques using Fibonacci ratios on both the time and price axis of the market. She has been a featured speaker on Fibonacci analysis for venues such as the Market Technicians Association, the Online Trading Expo, TradingMarkets, and Cornerstone Investments Group.

Ms. Boroden currently runs an intraday trading advisory/chat room service that includes end-of-day video updates focusing on Stock Index Futures. She mentors individuals on her analysis technique and also conducts group seminars on this same technique.

You can easily reach Carolyn Boroden for more information at: www.fibonacciqueen.com.